Power In the Pressure Cooker Frustration

By Chief Apostle M. III

No part of this book may be reproduced or transmitted in any form or by any means, electronic or mechanical including, photocopying, recording, or by any information storage and retrieval system without permission in writing from the author. Please direct you're inquires to chiefapostlem3@live.com.

Power In The Pressure Cooker - Frustration is a trademark of Established Leadership Designs, producing materials for Business & Leadership Development.

POWER IN THE PRESSURE COOKER - FRUSTRATION

ISBN-13: 978-1530348473
ISBN-10: 1530348471
Printed in the United States of America
Second Edition
Copyright © 2016, 2017 Chief Apostle M. III

Graphics: Digital Creations SCT
www.digitalcreationsct.com

Nous Mass Media
9494 Humble Westfield Rd. #432
Humble, Texas 77338
www.nousmassmedia.com

Copyright © 2016, 2017 by Chief Apostle M. III. All rights reserved
Printed in the United States of America

TABLE OF CONTENTS

Acknowledgments 5

Contributions 7

Introduction...9

Chapter 1...13

    Frustration; what is it?..13

Chapter 2..29

Passion; how do I get it and what's 'Passion'?....................29

Chapter 3..39

    Employment (The Occupation of Frustration)..........39

Chapter 4..59

    Purpose (The Purpose of Frustration)......................59

Chapter 5..81

    Expectancy...81

Chapter 6..93

    Live...93

Chapter 7...109

    Steps...109

Chapter 8...117

    The Literalness of Authenticity................................117

Chapter 9...127

    Twenty Times More..127

Chapter 10...137

Stopped in The Middle of The Road.................137

Chapter 11..151

Note, Notation(s) and Noteworthy...................151

Chapter 12..161

Stop!..161

ACKNOWLEDGMENTS

This part becomes very simple and very easy. Honoring others who have your best interest is an honored place to have. The people that give life to what is written cannot be neither denied nor dismissed. Such a valuable role each person portrays alongside each accomplishment. Truly deserving of each acknowledgment while working with and being in the trenches persevering until each project has been completed. I'm grateful for each person.

My very own newly started publishing company; Authors Prerogative Arts & Publishing Company? Chief Apostle M.III (Founder & C.E.O).

To my book cover designer, graphic artist consultant, and on this particular project; 'Prophetess Ja'da P. Hooks'. The 'Founder & C.E.O' of www.digitalcreationsct.com and also the owner of V2Fitness Studio and JaaSpa as a 'License Massage Therapist'@ V2fitnessstudio@gmail.com.

As acknowledgments are made there are other persons that are currently shadowing the success of each published work who will remain unmentioned until a more appropriate time. However, in my heart and in my life, they are precious. To Dr. Lovella Mogere, my publisher noumassmedia@gmail.com. Thank you once again.

Each person mentioned by name is assisting in the completion of this project as an assignment from eternity.

As an author I'm very grateful for my reading audience; you rock! I'm totally aware of your readership, following and purchasing of what is written, by this author.

CONTRIBUTIONS

To each supporter financially, without "God", without 'God's prompting' and without your complicit obedience not one of the things accomplished would have been possible.

Life has changed so much. There are multiple projects that have been enacted since my initial authorship of my first published books, "The Center Pages of Life Volumes1&2". My novice beginnings as an inexperienced writer, now turned author, into a more stable, established stage of authoring/authorship is a journey. From novice to a more mature experienced writer, turned author, the time spent in application has been well invested.

The opportunities that have presented themselves while being stretched as an author are not so difficult to accomplish. Every opportunity presented is an applicable learning curve if perceived properly and correctly. My learning curves even have learning curves as development takes place to personally become a more astute author. This application for learning more in the field of writing, authoring and authorship often expands so quickly. What has developed is an awareness. This is an awareness of multiple endeavors transpiring all at once.

My new website address: establishedleadershipdesigns.com will host a variety of topics geared towards 'Business & Leadership Development', 'Authorship' for new authors/writers and a host of other topics and my authored books; The Center Pages of Life Volumes 1&2 and other written works which will be available for purchase.

INTRODUCTION

Statements such as "change is inevitable", are probably world-renowned statements in every language and on every continent worldwide. The origination of this cliché and its life transforming phrase which without would be impossible. It is with expressions that reliefs are afforded and the anticipation of a brighter day that life is lived or futuristically maintained. So many other expressions can be included as hopeful solutions.

A different statement also surfaces, 'you can't see the forest for the trees'. The origin of the quote is unknown, but it implies the view being limited or blocked. When the view is blocked things that are already in existence become distorted. There are things presently, that are based upon not being able to see beyond what is presently blocking its view. How many beautiful moments that are now unattainable due to the inability to not 'see' their existence?

Classic arguments always complicate certain viewpoints by never giving proper perception to any truth. The arguments become very caustic and very disturbing. There are emotions which erupt when pressure is applied. Many individuals are hot headed, strong willed and

8

disproportionately unstable, never being certain about any circumstance. Others are 'flighty'; they are always 'flying by the seat of their pants'. Difficult people are not that difficult (hard) to find. Most often, it is the best ideal to leave people who are programmed as 'difficult' exactly where you find them. If you are not assigned to difficult people you will quickly learn that you are not. Exasperation will inform you that you are not assigned.

The thing that may appear as being extremely difficult to some maybe the extravagant forte of someone whose view is totally different. Grace (Divine Enablement) determines a lot. There are people who have learned to live a life of "rolling with the punches". Everything that takes place in their life is never challenged, changed or confronted. To live a life of 'merry go round the sunshine, merry go round the moon, merry go round the sunshine on every afternoon, 'boom', is not as nice as it seems. This only works in 'kids' world' or 'kiddie land', not in a mere world of opportunities, options and multiplied choices.

The pleasantries of innocence are absolute but those pleasantries eventually mature into adult people; however differently. "Here we go around the 'mulberry bush' works wonders when all of the little lassies and little lads cooperating while moving in the same clockwise circular motion in unison. At any given moment those persons participating can decide to change the clockwise rhythm of motion into a counterclockwise momentum, everyone is in trouble. Most assuredly when everyone is in sync they are taken unaware/by surprise. Everyone begins falling over the over person and sometimes falls upon the other individual. When this takes place, you hear some of the shouting of the other children, get off me, you hurt me and others are in tears crying hysterically while others are hostile and very angry attempting to find out what or who caused the fall.

Maybe, this is where you are! As you begin reading, let's journey together.

POWER IN THE PRESSURE COOKER FRUSTRATION

CHAPTER 1

FRUSTRATION; WHAT IS IT?

When engaged in a conversation it is often thought that the person with whom the conversation is held understands the words used without the need of defining. Words that are not defined are disturbing. The words are disturbing not only to the user but also to the one spoken to. Developing a vast and pronounce vocabulary is important. Understanding when to use your liturgy of words with its extensive vocabulary has an important place. Somethings that are constantly shared are meaningless to others. There appears to be a disconnect when shared. The disconnect is only normal chatter. Nothing serious distinguishes the conversation as any different to the one that it is shared. No one's interest is peaked. What is discussed bears no significance at all. Why should it be shared? What was shared only holds meaning to the one who shared. Various emotions begin to build within and to manifest outwardly.

The stage has now become set for 'Frustration'!

Incoherent speech without interpretation does not dispel any myths. This is such a deafening sound, knowing that no one is listening. Such statements unearth feelings of emotional distress; you're talking, and no one's listening. It is not based upon how much effort that is applied while attempting to gain the attention desired. There are constant attempts to see whose watching or who's looking as you desperately seek for their attention but appear completely invisible in their eyes.

This basic scenario gives way to the first chapter: 'Frustration'.

There is great anxiety taking place because of displaced actions. The insight that comes with a certain expose' are totally delightful. At the speed of light 'frustration' comes. Frustration is unrehearsed as everyone finds that moment when reality hits you. The reality that hits you like a truckload of bricks is that you are 'Frustrated'. The 'frustration' that you are experiencing today has lain dormant for years. Throwing bricks at glass houses never resolves dormant issues. The issues that lie dormant need to be addressed. However, when the unaddressed issues are refused the appropriate and proper confrontation, it only heightens and escalates the intensity of what is experienced.

Okay, so what is 'Frustration'?

Frustration – frustration is an alluding to an illusion of facts or factors throughout life that have not evolved nor have they come into existence. Frustration is the coddling aid of emotions which are typically unexpressed verbally. Frustration is viewed as gestures seen by multiple facial expressions. This is followed by subsequent, consistent body language.

Certainly, the definition for 'Frustration' listed is not the normal researched and accepted definition. The definitive liberty taken leaves room for more, and is not limit by its current definition. A different perception on, 'what is 'frustration' will be addressed. As this is addressed, you will have the option in life once again to breathe. There are many disadvantages to not knowing. The disadvantage of not knowing is disastrous. The responses of not knowing are ill advised. Life is constant in its awareness. Frustration presents foreboding threats with unplanned for events which present feelings of being helpless. Being overwhelmed does not only cause feelings of delusion but being overwhelmed also manifests symptoms of 'Frustration'. If the symptoms of frustration are not recognized, serious panic ensues with feelings of helplessness. As this is considered, let's have a little fun beginning now. A key symptom of frustration normally begins the domino effect. A key symptom is listed first. Other possible symptomatic expressions of frustration are listed. This listing is to personally evaluate the possibility of where you are or maybe what you continually experience without understanding that your key symptom is 'frustration'. As you read, the findings of your experience may vary, your expressions that you have experienced may be in multiple symptoms, not just one symptom alone. It would be nice if only eating a pizza was the remedy.

Have you ever attempted to understand frustration or more less people who are frustrated? The symptoms of 'Frustration' are numerous. I will outline a snapshot of varied symptoms.

The symptoms listed below are possible manifestations that you are possibly encountering as bouts of 'Frustration'. This is not written as a sad monologue, it is written to alert and to inform multiplied millions that their experiences are oftentimes motivational. Each level of motivation does not always initially surface as a motivator. We all experience this sideways way of thought and immediately begin struggling. Our struggle generally surfaces from different trains of thought. The train of thought learned surfaces as what we think that the answer is, sometimes it hurts more finding out that we are totally off track (train) with the training of thought which was passed generationally.

15

This is where troubleshooting becomes our conquistador enabling conquest or mastery at a place not trained (train of thought). With such possibility presented, an opportunity of mass proportions to displace history and to invasively replace history with something more. Innovation would be that premise for more. Do not allow the list below to daunt you. It is only a list, but you are the opportunist, presented with multiple opportunities. Take the challenge. Confront what needs to be confronted, make your move, change both time and lives. You're in the driver's seat, this is your moment not to only make things better, but to make things great; Master it! Great possibilities begin with endless adventures.

The first is the old soliloquy which shadows most, others follow depressions lead.

(1). Depression

(2). Paranoia

(3). Chaos

(4). Discouragement

(5). Restlessness

(6). Sleeplessness

(7). Constant Hostility

(8). Rudeness

(9). Regretfulness

(10). Uncontrolled Outbursts

(11). Anger (constant irritability)

(12). Incompatibility

(13). Jealousy

(14). Stealing

(15). Lying

(16). Cheating; various levels, not just infidelity

(17). Disgruntled Behavior

(18). Unbelief

(19). Unthankful

(20). Ungrateful

(21). Constant Complaining

(22). Disunity

(23). Disappointment(s)

(24). Incessant Grief

(25). Incessant Grieving

(26). Excessive Weight Gain (Obesity)

(27). Excessive Weight Loss (Bulimia)

(28). Erectile Dysfunction (Men)

(29). Loss of Sexual Interest (Women)

(30). Violence

The list on the previous page is an adventure listing. It is not an exhaustive retort of every symptom of frustration. There is a more detailed reaction that should be known about frustration. Being able to know the initial symptoms will help you avert many hurtful deviations now that you know what are some of the symptoms. Much has been misdiagnosed when it comes to the symptoms of

'Frustration. Many individuals are highly sedated with medical cocktails. Medicinal cocktails are the mixing of certain medicines that do not coagulate properly together. This has been the predominate culturally practiced ideology. Such would be known as the main prescribed solution for this undiagnosed, unrelated 'hypothesis'. The real needs are unacknowledged. However, with a correct answer, it is established as a solution; the individual's inability of expression. Through this, it is hindered by non-responsive innovative skills which lie dormant. They are unexpressed, untapped and unused. This primary reason for this is answerable, because to the individual who is frustrated, the things mentioned are unknown.

Frustration, is being in a dilemma and having no way out. It is an unforeseen forecast. This unforeseen forecast becomes the phobia that lurks in the dark, unwelcomed. Every facet of this waits for an opportune time to leap out of hiding. The dramatics of 'Frustration's' leap causes terror as a shriek of horror is belted out. It appears that at a certain juncture in life, the same thing repeats itself repetitiously repeatedly. This can be very disturbing and completely frustrating. For some, this appears as though it is planned. It is as if you are 'damned if you do' or 'damned if you don't'. Such an apparent place of quitting and giving up or so it seems, but honestly it is not the place or the time for either. You are exactly where you need to be as you read, "Power in the Pressure Cooker {Frustration}". Quitting as an option becomes a presented opportunity to everyone. The individuals excel, exceed and do well are the ones that do not take quitting's opportunity or quitting's giving up presentations. The successful person continues to persevere. It is unknown how close the door is to opening, as soon as persistency ceases the door 'opens'! ~Chief Apostle M.III~

If you quit, if you stop now, everything that you have endured, will have to be endured all over again; this is sheer torture. ~Chief Apostle M.III~

Only initially taking a reflective moment reflecting over your life you will find that the etch marks of frustration are deeply indelibly imprinted throughout your entire life without question. The quietness of a storm does not lessen its threat nor its impending danger or disastrous capability. The quieter a storm appears, the more disastrous the storm is upon impact. So many individuals are currently carriers. They are carriers of silent storms; known as, deadly frustrations. We learn to hide the feelings that are felt during childhood. The feelings of self-dejection surface later in life, with recognizable vengeance. Its havoc wreaking volatility expresses itself within every stratus of life with no regard for gender or skin ('hue') color. Certain fields of society will construct a reasoning, a certain rationale which will not afford an understanding of the purposed reasoning for the outbursts. These are uncontained and cannot be managed by the individual. The uncontrollable outbursts emotionally. The outbursts, consisting of the scars that internalized, silent frustration leaves in its wake of destruction. Silences inevitability endangers everyone. Silence with its threatening stranglehold, leaving its victim expressionless, expressionless in an attempt for self-implosion, while further categorizing helplessness through destructive behavior.

Every known cycle of self-destruction, self-destructive habits over time become normal although they are abnormal. The abnormality of destructive behavior is repeated, while clinically being diagnosed by most clinicians as normal aberrant behavior. This pseudo behavior, becomes adapted, learned, practiced, and applied to go unpunished or un-penalized. Factors surrounding and supporting such acts are formulated. The formulation takes place through medicinal means of treatment giving a free range of non-coherent activities which are dismissed as a result of the side-effects of prescription drugs. Many learn to adapt to a prescribed regimen of prescriptions in order to remain expressionless.

Life for most individuals is too hard. To others life is too long and attached with multiple responsibilities for which no plan is in place. People become overwhelmed. Some are so overwhelmed that senility sets in. As oppressive frustrations deeply seated within surface they surface with such an unruliness that the notion of addressing such frustrations become buried further inside. As ominous as this portrayal is the things portrayed can become more foreboding. This forecast does not finalize the obvious; you're "Frustrated"! When reality finally hits, you realize just how silently frustrated you've lived. Life does not guarantee roads that are pothole free. It is up to 'you' the driver to be aware of the potholes, attempting to avoid every pothole yet safely navigating.

As safe as you're driving while safely navigating, be advised, you will encounter, potholes. Uh oh, oops, you just hit one! That was completely humorous. But when you're frustrated, for some reason, funny, just doesn't seem, so funny. Maybe the possibility of you not wanting to acknowledge that you are frustrated is the reason there's no fun and no humor. The most difficult task to undertake is the task of frustration. Being frustrated can be hard, very hard; not wanting your frustration to be known and you're not acknowledging it, makes is even harder. Frustration always slips out when it is least expected.

To a person who's homeless, frustration is totally unavoidable. At best to the homeless person, it is completely totally embarrassing at best. To an unemployed person who has obligations that are pending, to that person frustration can be an unbearable weight. In a world filled with crazed individuals, in a world filled with uncertainty and a crisis of identity, frustration can become an overwhelming chain of events. A college student, cramming for exams after a long night of extreme partying, such a panic of emotions and classroom frustrations becomes a constant dilemma. The frustration, attempting to remember classes, attempting to remember courses, the chaotic influence of both senior, junior, freshman and sophomore 'peer pressure'. The peer influence of attempting to belong. The when and the where to fit in or do I fit in anywhere at all. These are the pressures that every person alive faces as life is attempted. No nationality is any different only the geography, topography is breathtaking. The same pressures are presented.

Can you imagine leaving one country or nation expecting to lead a better life only to find that the nation or the country that you migrated from was better than the country or the nation that you immigrated to. This would be very disappointing. It would incur deep sadness, loneliness and dreadful frustration. Such deep dissatisfaction surfaces as the reality of how far away from home, your original nation and country you are. Geographically, you are in a new nation with new people that you are possibly completely unacquainted with. The new people, the unlearned language or languages necessary to communicate stir deep fear and panic within you. A panic and a fear that you've never experienced. Your silent wish and your silent prayer is that they will not harm you nor the others with whom have traveled. Frustration now has reached a new pitch unheard of with such a frequency level within that tears begin forming and ever so softly grace your cheeks, but inside you are paranoid. Inside you are screaming, but no one hears anything, only you and your inner 'frustrations'.

I'm quite certain that without hesitation after this initial hardship, 'you can now, sing 'Annie get your gun'.

Undoubtedly your true objective for being in a different country/foreign nation is the dream of making life successful. The dream that you have held dear to included making it better for your family. Perhaps you have left family members or better yet; they are with you. This can become very difficult, when everyone's looking for you to save them from every difficulty. Now you are their savior, you now become their hope. If nothing happens, their heart becomes sick, their hopes are dashed. If everything happens on a positive note, they flourish as a bewildered tree that comes back to life. There is nothing greater than when frustrations turn into positive revealing's'.

Calls of distress are continually sent out, but are infrequently heard and not given attention. This similarity borders upon frustration as desperation sets in. Countless individuals send out distress calls daily. Most calls of distress are taken for granted, often shrugged off as 'maybe he/she' is just having a 'moment'. The moments that were dismissed have often become the midday news breaking report or maybe the five to six o'clock evening news, even possibly a newsflash feed. It is fatally tragic if lives are lost. It is so horrifying to receive a report that the person that was having their moment, ended their own life. Something different, something new must take place.

Frustrations cannot be avoided.

Frustrations must not be avoided.

The seriousness of trying to avoid frustration has revealed itself as apathetic and completely delusional. No one alive has anticipated what's next or possibly, the disturbing outcome. The mountain seems bigger than it is and larger than it needs to be. Its appearance is as though society staged continuing reports of distress, continuing reports of tragedy, travesties, even moments of deep anguish. The trepidation that this perpetuates is disturbing. People continually cave under the normal pressures which life presents. Frustration, after all is not your enemy. The enemy is, not knowing how to handle nor direct frustration. Now this, becomes your enemy. A greater unknown happens when knowledge is improperly applied or where there is a lack of knowledge. Daily distress, daily distressed people running at the speed of light, but completely ending in darkness. Everyone, for some unknown reason ends up as a pundit or as a puppet of 'Frustration'. With no seeming way of escape, multitudes scream out in sheer panic being horrified at the grip of 'Frustrations' grasp upon their heart. Their lives become utter ruin to outrun the inner turmoil of their own personal life/lives of frustration.

Is this the fatal path of frustration or is frustration devised or presented with other options? What's placed on the table is placed on the table for our choosing to select something different, something better. This is a place without fear to fail, nor the fear of failing or failure. If this was only designed for fatalism, we must all die at once! Unfulfilled expectations are not designed to die at the grasp of "Frustrations" grip.

The grip of 'Frustrations' grasps is only an indication 'that you have been chosen'. No, not chosen to fail, but chosen to achieve successfully. Everything in life experiences 'Frustration'. Most would like to conclude 'frustration' as distress or undue duress. Whatever the choice you choose in assisting you in being able to accept frustration as your definition choice, be sure to know that 'Frustration' improperly directed destroys. Frustration improperly directed, destroys hope, dreams, visions of grandeur i.e. lavish lifestyles, it destroys lives, livelihood investment; it also destroys families, homes, marriages and many other things both personal and interpersonal. It is important to understand that this is not the original intent or the assignment for "Frustration". Frustrations assignment must personally be reassigned its assignment. The reassignment of 'Frustration' takes place through thoughtful, thorough, insightful application.

Understanding is vital with this level of process. Not knowing what is applicable in frustrations fury does not help. The need to know what it takes to redirect the negativity of frustration will save the lives of countless individuals. As assuredly as you know that you are breathing, the need for something more will happen. When you become aware that there is something more to this virtue of frustration, the possibility of many seasons, seeming like lifetimes will have taken place. Don't fret! The seasons have passed, but the lifetime that you have been given is just beginning. Everything that was experienced, everything that has crossed your path, has only prepared you. The transit has aided in your readiness, it has set you up and prepared for this. It is "Passion". Frustration generates and creates dominant "Passion". Not only does 'Passion' relate to 'Frustration', but 'Passion' is "Frustrations" best friend and at other times, frustrations arch nemesis. Frustration and passion should be identified as completely identical twins without speculation. The push of 'Frustration' into the welcoming open arms of "Passion"!

In the same womb frustration and passion appear to relate, but this embryonic unknown language or conversation held between the two is indescribable.

Frustration: Frustration whispers to passion with an unforgettable dialogue.

The dialogue goes something like this.

Passion, when we are released out of this dark place, (the womb), remember, I go first. I will be born first. I will begin the labor pains to have us both expelled.

Passions response is, ok, I will remember.

Passion asks frustration, we are a team, right? Passions dialogue continues, because all of this that we have been through together, I don't want to ever be without you or not be able to understand your cues when you give them.

Frustration states you will always know my cues. You will know when you are to enter in, and when to make your way to the stage, and your entrance into, 'the play of life'.

CHAPTER 2

PASSION; HOW DO I GET IT AND WHAT'S 'PASSION'?

The details of a risqué photograph or a painting and the embellished ravenous features presented send shockwaves of rapid impulse through most inciting purposeful passion innately.

In my quaint observation as I observed unwittingly without any logical attempt in so doing; I came across a word graphic statement regarding, 'Passion'. In my humble opinion, I directly disagree with its stated definition applicably. However as with all good writers and authors certain things are presented as drama or as speculative, others, more so as factual none the less. I will allude to my findings while including what I discovered. My discovery is covered in my next sentence. Passion is derived from a Latin word, meaning to suffer. if you genuinely love something you suffer for it. ~ Unknown

Here is our observation. The interjecting of the word 'to suffer' and not the word 'suffer' only. This introduction of suffering is based upon adverse conditions. Most likely the conditions are experienced in a dreaded atmosphere. Suffering is always unwelcomed, and suffering is more likely of a drastic nature. While we understand that not all suffering is the same, this reference does to some degree shed light upon the various shades and meanings that suffering implies. Yet it is the term 'suffer, suffering, and to suffer' that scares the hebegebees out of most of us. Yeah right, who in their right mind wants voluntarily "to suffer", not just 'suffer'? 'To suffer'; rightly means to 'put up with or to allow by giving permission'. I'm careful as we tread on the precious ground of 'Passion'. The accepted place of passion is more generally reserved for intimacy or intimate interaction in private between two consenting adults. Normally this 'Passion/Acts of Intimate Passion' is sexual in nature. There are other acts that are just as passionate although they are criminal in nature known as, 'Acts of Passion'.

The acts that are related to 'Passion' need clarity. Every act of 'Passion' does not have criminal intent. I'm certain that no one desires 'to suffer' violence as an act of anyone's

'Passion' especially if they are the target of such heinous acts which beggar description. So now we view the possibility of 'Passion' being corrupted. Perversions of any truth are possible if the mind accepts it as being normal and the practice of it begins as a normal lifestyle. So where do the lines begin? What is normal and why? Are there acceptable forms of "Perverted Passion" that we 'suffer' or is all 'Passion' put into the same category? While reading, please feel free to proverbially, 'chime in'. From a personal perspective please give us your view of 'Passion'. Everyone loves the heat of 'Passion' when love is involved. Should passion be a place of 'suffering'? If passion is to be a place of suffering to what degree should passion and suffering or to 'suffer' be allowed?

If such internal bravery takes place other questions arise. Certainly, questions arise as you are reading. Perhaps the thoughts that arise are personally unmentionable thoughts, perhaps. There is possibly a part of you that has a 'yet'. This 'yet', are the things that you have not experienced. They are the things that you have not given thought to nor consideration, as of 'yet'. Be very sure that those thoughts will, but they have not 'yet'. The proper 'passion' is an armor bearer for 'frustration'. While over time passion and frustration begin to merge as one. The connecting of 'frustration' and 'passion' are unequalled, not coincidental. Enterprises blossom when both are in motion.

The two may not personally be known as co-equals but they

are sure to be co-existent. If you are trying to explain away the frustration and passion that you feel, your task to explain away either will be very difficult. To attempt to explain either away is as though breathing without air is possible or living as a human being without blood is doable. Neither application works. Breathing, air, blood coursing throughout your body as a human is not possible if they first do not co-exist. There is the absolute necessity of each working together as a unit of one. Throughout "Power in the Pressure Cooker (Frustration)" your very resolve will be actively tested. Your very resolve will be tested for very good reasons as you read more indepth. This is a defining moment. Let's discuss 'Passion' and how passion is derived.

Lacking momentum personally is a perfect example of passion missing. But what contributed to the lack of 'passion'?

The question above is one that should be asked frequently, personally. A lack of 'Passion'! The complex values of passion are somewhat confusing.

At what point did life become mundane and the desire to breathe non-existent?

Has there has been a conflicting battle greater than your choice of offense?

Was this the bearer of bad news?

Has this become anything otherwise less acceptable?

Once intense desire is lost, what should be expected?

Passion is a forte' of all things possible. Passion is not an option. In life, 'Passion' to survive should not be your only objective, there should also be the passion to thrive successfully. You cannot succeed successfully without 'Passion'!

What is the object that you cherish which has created a fire within your bosom with desire?

How intense is this desire?

Cherished desire with intensity relate to 'Passion' like air to breath, escalating an insanely intense brush fire which refuses extinguishing. ~ Chief Apostle M.III~

The debilitating facts are, you're "Frustrated"! Frustration is the key to awakening 'Passion' at any level when principles brought to light that are well understood.

What's 'Passion'?

In our beginning dialogue 'Passion' is defined as 'meaning to suffer'. This is derived from a supposed 'Latin' origin but also is implied in the 'Greek' language as well. Coincidently an example is attached to this definition. The example is; if you love something you 'suffer' for it.

Every person alive also lives 'Frustrated' at some point. The degree of frustration that each person experiences is different. Frustration must begin being viewed from a different angle presently not perceived. Frustration is not harmful. The method of frustration becomes harmful when frustration is carried out without reason. Before you begin acting out or taking out your frustrations or acting upon your 'frustration(s)', know your frustrations origins. Knowing the origin of something is not only based upon where it originated, but why it originated.

Passion is initially an intense longing; whether the longing is satiable or insatiable, it is longed for. This intense longing is not only intimately directed but this intense longing can also be used as a driving force. Passion is such a driving force that if set in sync, passion produces great accomplishments, with great accolades consisting of goal setting. With every positive, there is a developing negative awaiting, with every negative there is a developing positive. Nothing is as it seems. It appears that we are living in an auto virtual world, so it appears. We must capture the forces of antiquity refusing to be antiquated. The structure of life with varying lifestyles has fueled society, while having insufficient evidence. Such insufficient evidence fueled, not knowing that there are truths offsetting certain actions. The inability to afford passion without payment is wonderful although passion itself does have an expense plan. It is all free; something for nothing is not a valid affordability, anywhere. In life, there will always be costs.

At whose expense are the cost?

Nothing is literally free; an expense is always attached. An unknown price tag does not negate the fact that there was a transaction. Such is Passions' price. Passion is not free!

At others expense an investment has been made on your behalf. The interactions are time consuming. The interactions develop value as they are consistently practiced, being put into their proper place.

Passions intermixing of mutual exchanges is volatile!
~ Chief Apostle M.III

Passion can quickly turn into frustration if passion is ever dismissed, if passion is taken for granted, if passion is only casually taken as a pastime with no further significance. If passion is gestured with no reciprocation, this type of non-reciprocal passion can be unhealthy. One of the deepest depictions of frustration that can ever be experienced is to be involved where there is no passion. When there is constant frustration at some point a celebration and a romantic dance is needed. Each day the grind of life is designed to stop what is special. This must be restored in those moments that are sensitive and celebrative to ensure that the beauty of each moment is restored, and refreshed, not lost. Tranquility is great but always remember tranquility is not without passions price. To acknowledge tranquility, chaos was first known.

Chaos's character is yet a diverted form of frustration laced with subtle amounts of passion. Frequently, the cues of injustice are missed as frustration takes over blindsiding its recipient. Certain phenomenons go unnoticed and unchecked when passion takes over and frustrations voice diminishes.

In view of the above, how perfectly placed are your fears when things do not go the way you expected? Panic always builds upon frustration whenever it can go unchecked. However, frustration never goes unnoticed. An attempt to hide frustration is like an attempt to not quarantine illnesses that are harmful to everyone. The similarities of passion and frustration are so intertwined. The rabid animal is frustrated. Its frustration is shown by the anger (snarling) that is portrayed. The snarling is very passionately displayed, but it is also deadly if a victim is subjected to its frustration. Surprisingly, frustrations are one of 'The Birthing Places of Complaints and Ideas'. For a shrewd awakening, there are stressed out pregnant people in their last month (trimester).

Every thought of being without passion is also an uncertainty of cause. The cause of being without a place to give birth. Unenviable parts of this is based upon the frightening experience of frustration that most people personally encounter. Once conceived the acknowledgment of bringing something into existence wisely is at times challenged. The challenge is viewed by the degree of complaints and the manifestation of ideas. This develops a unique launching pad or springboard for 'Passion'. In layman's terms, this is where 'Passion' is developed and defined in non-negotiable terms. It is where your private world meets your personal world articulately, knowledgeably in terms that you understand. Acquiring passion should not be your principal concern but keeping passion. Many answers are formulated in private. However, the answers do not seem to be forthcoming because they are laced and disguised as questions.

Finalizing this portion, how is passion derived?

Passion's motivations can be derived from the need to vindicate, from the need to avenge or the need to seek revenge. This preponderance ascribes itself in every point of preference, in each attempt to silence certain schisms or to silence beliefs. With great latitude taken, these may have been used against you, spoken against you, your family or perhaps others within your circle of life. When things are portrayed by others as a real forecast overshadowing your life unknowingly stirring and activating an incredible assignment within you that you feel compelled to prove wrong.

This assignment burns day and night within your being creating a volume of force and passion that is urgent in its fulfillment as though an extreme emergency has occurred; and it has. There are keys to fulfilling any assignment. The keys begin with every idiosyncrasy; every frustration and with every passion. Passion can remove every conscious fear possessed. As frustration presses upon you, you want to pursue more, you want to be more, than mediocre or the norm. Every person can be mediocre while hinging on the doorway of the norm. This, is not what you are called to do, for, nor to be.

Is it important to possess both passion and frustration? Yes, it is important to possess both.

CHAPTER 3

EMPLOYMENT (THE OCCUPATION OF FRUSTRATION)

Who hired you? If you are ever asked this question, the tense tone of this question signifies its depth and its serious nature. The person asking this question may have engaged a certain level of sensitivity based upon how well you left your prior place of employment or not possibly exposing deep trouble, if you are just beginning a new job, possibly a change of vocation. This completely new beginning of school and the whole description of expectations and requirements, your whole day can quickly go into a downward spiral. When this takes place, many individuals subject themselves to depression; depressions visitation is not short lived for most. A most vital point must be stated.

The quickest solution to any problem is to occupy the problem, put the problem to work. Give the problem, the occupation, employment. Distract the problem by occupying and employing it. If the problem lacks employment, it only creates greater frustration if not occupied. We are familiar with the clichéd phrase of 'you have too much time on your hands'. This is not a contradiction. Successful individuals employ time, not only time management. All of the evidence in the world cannot contradict being busy. Being busy does assist if frustration persists, but being busy alone does not resolve everything.

Frustration is not your enemy, frustration discovers your creativity and reveals it to you; this includes your purpose. ~Chief Apostle M.III~

Being employed begins an assent and it also establishes differences while allowing a proper dispensing of energy and creativity. Employing frustrations is not an easy task. It is possible to employ your frustrations. You can employ your frustrations and even profit while doing so. The overwhelming burden that accompanies frustrations is not imaginative, it is real. However, with that reality great insight is often missed. Great insightfulness often accompanies desperation. During the initial stage, the obvious takes place. The obvious becomes very challenging.

What is the obvious?

The obvious is a face to face brush with life. Most are

acquainted with a differing statement. Often it is not spoken of as a face to face brush with life, but instead as a face to face brush with death. Things are totally different when life is challenged or when life challenges you. A different perspective is needed when the obvious takes place.

It is possible to have a face to face brush with life and come away victorious. Considering how humans operate, if the brush is not dramatic enough (a face to face brush with death) most only consider the empathy that trades places. The empathy is how dire a situation became and how close to death they were. If only this perspective could be altered for a moment being replaced with how close to life, they were instead. The whole scenario would completely change. How common place it is to have a drama team; the onlookers for a funereal standing in the wings awaiting the eulogy of uncertainty, not the life of its victim. When a report is given of how tragic or how dire the situation has become and taken a turn for the worse, people gather their containers, their long-awaited bucket of tears grieving effortlessly over what they considered impossible as a loss. Who is willing to rush forward and stop the mourners; alerting the mourners to cease mourning while assessing each person's brush with death differently. At other times, things can be very overwhelming.

What has been viewed is not as it always appears.

When pressure is applied, in life most individuals do not

handle the pressure that is applied correctly. The facts which indicate that pressure is necessary are unknown. It is also unknown that pressure must be applied correctly to every situation. If the benefits from pressure are to be received, a certain level of application discomfort is involved. The usual subconscious action by most is irritability. This irritability spills over to frequent disorientation, possibly even incoherent actions as the pressure is applied.

The pressure mentioned refers to the frustration of the moment. A vast number of individuals will attempt to be strong being under great duress only to realize that the application used is the wrong application when dealing with stress or frustration. There is a great need to employ your frustrations adequately as a gift given to you from as a present from 'time' itself.

Please do not trivialize this.

Your greatest successes will take place when the insightfulness of employing your frustrations becomes second nature, like breathing. I cannot overstate the fact or the need to "employ your frustrations", occupy them. Occupying your frustrations and employing them does not legitimize anything that is illegal or immoral.

When frustrations are mentioned an unspoken remedy or solution is to allow yourself the liberty of taking the edge off by engaging in casual sex. Others their relief from stress, becomes drugs, others involve themselves in an alcoholic drinking binge attempting to escape life or the frustration that life has caused for them sends them into an eventful tirade. Others vent through hostility, acts of violence or hurtful words. The more drastic the measures are only lead to manipulation whenever you're not sure of how to employ your frustrations. The uneventful tirades only express the need for frustration to be gainfully employed. A correct position of frustration puts to work the seething hostilities, and occupies. Multiple endeavors are misdirected when the silence of frustration is in the room.

The conscious need to verify frustration and even arrest it is important. Once your frustrations have you held hostage, panic stricken and self-deprived with a muzzle you will find yourself completely immobilized. You must honestly and earnestly work your way out of this. Even as you begin working (employing and occupying your time) gainfully investigating what has ensnared you so completely. When your frustrations become the monitor of your day and of your night life truly seems hopeless, lost and completely impossible to navigate successfully.

If frustration takes you by the hand, it monitors your time by manipulating you causing you to grope aimlessly into the dark. If frustration captures you, it sedates, putting you to sleep snuffing the life out of you.

Frustration can be monstrous!

However as monstrous as frustration is, it can be conquered and permanently detached.

The purpose for "Power in The Pressure Cooker" {FRUSTRATION} being written is why you must recommend this book to others or purchase copies for someone you know who needs this for their own personal triumph.

When personal frustration reaches its highest point is the time limitations are lifted with success becoming the results. People are normally not hired without certain requirements being met. The potential new hires need experience, developed skillsets. This is what takes place in differing stages of frustration.

You do the hiring.

If you hire, you can fire.

This development of what you choose to give your time to is extremely important.

There are not very many people who will 'Fire' themselves especially knowing that most people believe that they are doing the best job that they can do. It is easy to believe this when you are not willing to address your frustration.

Pent up frustration(s), are not always 'Sexually' appeased.

There are frustrations which can exist. The individual is aware of being capable although their clear choice is to be non-compliant, choosing not to do more or better. Their choice has been made to remain as though incapable. This develops into a complex, the complex of the shifting of blame upon the next person, but not accepting responsibility for their inactivity.

Our current society is filled with individuals who lovingly and even joyously blame others for their lack of fortitude. As this take place, it offsets the ability of the one blamed. Every stage of life becomes the culprit constantly offsetting their productivity while altering the contributions in life that they are personally capable of making.

Most people are not angry with others, their anger is self-directed. To have opportunities presented, lucrative opportunities presented and to not take advantage of wholesome opportunities is infuriating and frustrating.

Opportunities are often missed because of an inability to employ them.

This is where the truth sets you free, and where the rubber meets the road. I'm sure that you're in agreement as you recall multiple opportunities that you were afforded but you denied employing. It is amazing how life-long opportunities that were presented can alter your life. Missed opportunities can create a bitter and difficult perspective about life once they are missed. Every opportunity should be studied thoroughly.

Each opportunity should not be hastily accepted and should not hastily be entered until you have all the facts and all the facts are squarely placed on the table. If an opportunity is presented and you do not have quietness within begin to search out the reason that quietness within does not exist. Oftentimes this does not mean the opportunity presented has no legitimacy but the conclusion can be that you are stretched beyond what you are normally accustomed. However, in each instance be sure that you have peace of mind. Be sure that your heart is at peace once you've completed a thorough search, having researched everything before a decision is reached or finalized.

Let's stretch our imagination for a moment. In all truthfulness, you did not miss another opportunity presented to you. Everything is completely 'Employed'! You have mastered every "Frustration" giving it a precise and proper occupation. You have learned how to master every attempt to cause you frustration, also you have embraced key principles of insightfulness, now having knowledge of what to do, if frustration shows up. Knowing that if any degree of frustration surfaces that it only manifests because it is bored and needs occupancy (an occupation). Frustrations seat is defeated within as you have mastered both its sound and its method. At each interval, you occupy your frustrations.

Occupying or Employing your frustrations does not mean that you have to work. However, being assured of how to work, occupy and employ your frustrations as you create a definitive portfolio with your new insightfulness. If

45

frustration is not properly employed and given a productive occupation, frustration becomes totally overwhelming.

In the laboratory of life everyone can experiment. Each experimentation that happens must be wisely chosen. Choosing each life experiment wisely not only saves lives, yours especially but it saves time. There are experiments that will surface. Each experiment will surface as ideas seeming harmless but they are the casualties of life affecting numerous people and generations to come. Whatever you choose for yourself is based upon your driven need to outrun or to outdo your inner frustration. There is something that you need to prove to someone about something that has been negatively stated concerning you, your life, your possible accomplishment plus your future.

How difficult it has become to outdo and to outrun your inner frustrations. Those inner urgencies must be addressed. The best way to address those inner urgencies is to employ them. Give your inner urgencies an occupation. As you allow others to follow your success that you have mastered of your genius in their eyes. You know become and influencer, a master, a life coach and a voice of reason to the masses.

This is not only a stretch of the imagination. What's mentioned is possible. If you will do the impossible, you can stimulate the achievable. Your next question is, but how do I do the impossible? It is good that you have continued this inquiry. Prepare for the answer. Everyone's future is completely bright with promise. Do not allow anyone to tell you differently. Now to answer your question.

How do you do the impossible?

The impossible is most likely human logic, speculation and ironic probability. When things appear to be impossible, a slight degree of hesitation and fear are experienced. What you are experiencing is life. Life experiences including hesitation is normal. The degree of hesitation is given as a moment to reflect before deciding. This is a very necessary moment to move forward and to invest wisely before acquiescing what has been presented. Once you are clear internally as you check the gages of human logic, speculation and ironic probability, safe passage is required. Now your actions are needed. It is time to enact upon what was previously impossible but now is certainly achievable.

The deep stimulation of achievability is now present and presented to you as you move past what was previously a distraction. If the actions necessary, are not taken, you will find yourself operating in futile frustration.

The envelope is full of frustration (wealth and possibility) only spendable if you are willing to convert it into the current economies recognized accepted currency. Oh, by the way, remember the envelope is full. It is yours; use it wisely.

It is not only frustrating knowing that you have everything you need to be better but to have it and to not know how to use it (employ) or to further the wealth of its occupation ends disastrous. Not only will you find regrets so deeply that nothing can fill, but the contemplations of hopelessness will occupy some degree or parts of your life until indecisiveness ends, and actions to do begin. No one has ever not face trepidation (fear) with any project. The only difference between you and your frustration is that the other person faced fear, mistrust and frustration only to succeed. Every human being always has the same possibilities given. It is what you choose to do with the possibilities given to you that makes the difference.

The same creator, created all of creation!

No one is literally born with a silver spoon in their mouth. The greatest distance for some is from their hand to their mouth. ~Chief Apostle M.III~

Accessibility to acquire wealth is given to everyone. However, an elitist mentality stifles most; the elitist does not have it all.

There are disadvantages to being born with a proverbial silver spoon (a wealth ticket) in your mouth. A disadvantage can occur if you do not use the silver spoon to your advantage. Another disadvantage would be to not understand the need of a having a system of checks and balances. If the disadvantages are not noted, you can become exactly like the individuals who are not as privileged. Having a silver spoon mentality without possessing the proper business acumen and education becomes a complete waste. Individuals birthed into wealthy families are immersed into the understanding of how important it is to pass on generational wealth, successfully.

Test which are administered before an inheritance is given becomes a valued safety net. Each test should be simple, but, with great attention given while closely monitoring how the inheritor handles their passions, emotions and frustrations. This determines maturity and how well or how poorly the inheritor handles wealth and responsibilities.

Never decide to transfer family wealth without the proper supervisory provisions being solidly set in place. If the provisions or the stipulations are not met nor adhered to wait until the inheritor has positively proven themselves. This safely safeguards your family's generational wealth successfully.

It is in the heart of every successful parent to leave something of lasting value. This is also the desire of even the poorest and most destitute.

Tenacity is a virtue that must be caught by observation. Tenacity cannot be taught! ~ Chief Apostle M.III~

Tenacities ridiculous surge of relevance is based upon consistency. This establishes the ability of seeing the impossible from its onset until its completion. Once completed, your view of seeing things as impossible totally diminishes. Being inconsistent never brings anything to completion. Inconsistency only leaves etchings. These etch marks only serve notice that you are capable of more. They leave you hoping for more, but always doing and settling for less. It is not impossible to have hopes and to do nothing.

What does your future hopes consist of?

This question should send chills up and down your spine while stoking a morally competitive fire within your heart not allowing anything to deter nor detour you away from what you aspire to accomplish and what you're inspired to complete. Your frustrations should cause you to put everything on the table and face all of your inadequacies that you have believed about yourself. No, do not stop there. Once faced schedule a test not only a meeting (face off). The scheduled test should prompt indepth personal questioning. Choose to begin your test by asking yourself, how did I get here (in this current condition)? What will it take to remove myself from this non-positive, unproductive place?

Are you willing to take the challenge of "Employment" and to take the challenge of establishing the very rules of "Occupational Engagement"?

The challenges of employment can be a very bewildering place. The challenges become more pronounced, especially if you are seeking a certain level of employment while awaiting others to employ you. It becomes most hurtful, when you will not employ yourself. This is a defining moment. Now, it is honestly the 'Challenge of Employment'; the awaiting of others to employ you. The 'Job' is not what you need. What you literally need is the employing and occupying of what makes you 'you', that is, absolutely what you need without thought and without fail.

Quit doubting yourself!

Remember the only reason you are where you are presently 'is' because you are 'Angry'. All anger does not reveal itself as violent or vindictive. Anger can be healthy if it is established as a "Positive Passion" and interlaced with a pure objective. After all, the majority of what you're experiencing is only "Frustration". The feeling of frustration has become very unproductive. One simple reason that this feeling of frustration does not produce your desired results, is, your frustration has never been challenged or faced.

The emotion of frustration is set up in most of our lives as, 'Disappointment'. Undoubtedly the disappointment has stemmed from something which was promised or expected that never happened.

"Occupational Engagement" is a form of employment considered to be an occupation but if left unchecked, it kills' accomplishments, and it destroys future possibilities with promising engagements. You cannot allow your fears or the need for personal confrontation to abort nor to sidetrack your possibilities based upon your internal frustration. The possibilities of this taking place will constantly resurface until you choose to silence them through confrontation. I think that our greatest fear is not the fear of others but the fear of losing ourselves through greater accomplishments and achievements.

The reference, 'ourselves', is that which we have become comfortable, and complacent. It is the same comfortability with whom you've introduced others to and by such have become just as complacent. In a world of different sorts, we have become pigeonholed into a place of being mediocre, only an acceptance among many familiar acquaintances.

The obvious expectations of people are that you continue to be who you have presented yourself. Time changes, so do people and life. ~ Chief Apostle M.III~

There are 'Jobs' and there are 'Occupations'. All jobs are not occupations and all occupations are not jobs. Certain employed measures only force you to waste skill and time, but they do not employ you within. The necessity of an occupation helps and develops your skills often employing your talents without wasting your time or your skill. Frustrations are curtailed within this arrangement bringing great satisfaction. Being dissatisfied only reflects the fact that there is something more to you than meets the eye.

The 'Eye' of advancement is an opportunistic approach to achievement. Being able to perceive what's next through a panoramic scope of view is eye opening. In the time that it takes others' years to decide there are certain individuals who only take moments/minutes to make the same decision benefitting in the process. The ability to process so swiftly should be common. It should be as easy as what is next or normal to each person alive.

It is important to find the inner details of knowing what causes such rapidity of development within, in 'The Eye of Advancement'.

Inner curiosity will always stimulate advancement.

This inner curiosity assists in leaving a clean slate behind for those who will become your understudy. Being aware of how inner curious we all are does not develop anything negative. The negative is developed during the period of inner curiosity if left unchecked. If left unchecked, inner curiosity can be developed; not having healthy moral restraints thereby triggering lawlessness. However, there is no need to fear what innocent levels of curiosity create. What our frustrations afford us are choices.

This is where inner curiosity unchecked scares the living daylights out of us.

Each person's awareness for such inner curiosity/inner inhibitions has become maddening or has gone imaginatively wild. Therefore, with this, should the understudy determine not to take the clean slate left behind the understudy will find themselves at the same crossroads. The understudy at the least, coming to the same conclusions having dismissed what was left behind which was designed for the understudy to build and advance upon. The clean slate appears empty but the clean slate is not as it appears. It is full of prior experiences. It is full of experiments, with multiple attempts which can be accounted as being successfully accomplished, if the 'eye of advancement' is applied.

Frustration can be pictured as a progression of thought which is seemingly prideful. The progression of thought can be complete obstinate not willing to build upon something that they did not originate. To the frustrated there is no glory. There is no flowery glory in the developing continuation of something that had no initial origination of their creating.

That age-old nemesis that withstands humanity and times can be your worst nightmare; jealousy! ~ Chief Apostle M.III~

How frequently does this visitor prowl while all are visited from this age-old nemesis?

Everyone wants to do everything without assistance refusing the help that allows advancements to smoothly transition. The job becomes more intense and insanely difficult when experienced help is deferred and possibly denied. It is the occupations efficiency when the right assistance is accepted. Maybe a dream has your name in lights, but if lights do not exist you can only dream of your name being put in the stars. Hollywood maybe calling you but to answer the call from 'Hollywood' some type of telecommunication device needs to be invented. No horses, no advancement.

There are multiple advancements which stemmed from unproductive situations as people were hard pressed, searching for answers to make life easier. Internally they search for answers, seeking creation to afford them some sort of reprieve, finally the reprieve occurs. A dream takes place, a quick vivid idea (a glimpse of thought) takes place to advance their occupation making the job easier and the occupation that they have chosen a joy. Talk about occupied territory for them it joyously is just such, their territory is clearly occupied.

So many reasons are given to quit, to throw in the towel, to not advance another further (another step that is). It's not as easy to quit as you consider it is to quit. There will always be that nagging edge of thought. Should I have continued or just how close was I to accomplishing, completing or finishing? The questions never go away if you stop or quit too soon. For some it will never be known. Being a quitter/being a loser can constantly eat away at you for life if you do not receive adequate inspiration and empowerment.

Knowing what excites you is key to your accomplishments. It is 'what' excites you not 'who'! Others may assist in your assignment but others are not responsible for your fulfillment. You are the only individual responsible for your fulfillment and the completion of your assignment. No one knows internally when you are certain about your assignment but you. No one knows what fulfills you internally and when that internal fulfillment has been reached but you. There is a vast difference in knowing and fulfilling.

Lives are lost all too frequently based upon the demands that we place upon others. The lives that are lost take place when the gages of our life are broken and no longer readily readable. The barometric pressure from our life makes demands for what only we can attain/maintain, not others. The permanence of a moment is not as permanent as anticipated if no long-term plan is afforded or in place.

Milk that is spilled will either evaporate over time or will be ingested as a meal by a hungry pet while also attracting other smaller visible and invisible (undetected by the human eye) pests/insects in an urgent appeal to fulfill and to satisfy their longing with the presented opportunity. Most certainly at some point the spilled milk will be wiped or mopped away cleaning the area clearly leaving no trace of its once spilled area. The memory of the spilled milk and the momentary distress of its spill will also fade. In each instance, there were strange similarities taking place. The similarities were unalterable but nothing sociably different was noticed. What transpired is subconsciously noted but not normally obvious. This is what is described as unnoticeable. Every event was preceded by an act/an action (s) not normally noted. The spilled milk presented an occupation described as an opportunity but disguised to most as work (employment). We normally stress at things that are not as obvious or opportune at the time. It is impossible to see their wealth potential now. It is normally viewed as a serious and a grave error. This serious grave error throws individuals into panic or temper tantrums. As a result, outbursts of anger, scolding, and swear words are used. All of this happens because we cannot fine the proper way of viewing that moments rightful place or its value. In a not so conscious attempt, there is an attempt to figure out where each event fits, and what's the profit margin or is there profitability from every event experienced.

Unfortunately, this often-accidental scheduling of events releases a completely differing arrangement, creating an occupation for employment. Instead of embracing a negative slant, take the opportunistic approach. Find a way to take your frustration(s) to the bank; you have now become your own 'Entrepreneur'.

Nothing can ever keep you away from the opportune moments that are precisely yours and yours alone. Navigate, stretch forth, take over and take advantage, this is your very own adventure. Check it out, don't tread lightly, tread deeply!

CHAPTER 4

PURPOSE (THE PURPOSE OF FRUSTRATION)

Why does everything have to be about 'Purpose'? Does this sound angry and frustrated enough? Can things just happen just for the sake of happening; sheesh. Does this sound raunchy enough to be hostile begetting antipathy for a future rebuttal further entrenched into what is the ancient obvious? Frustrated huh, can't seem to keep your head off the ground and your feet stuck in the air, right?

Well join the club of rational reasoners who do the same! We are in this together with you 'Bud'. Are you ready for some "Fooootttttballl"; yep this is being done just to humor you...Is this annoying enough? This is just a limited feeling of how it is to live life aimlessly, only following the crowd; annoyed.

Passion without 'Purpose' is literally a virtual disaster waiting to happen figuratively, and it will. ~ Chief Apostle M.III. ~

The disaster of waiting?

Really, wait a minute. Is there really such a thing as the disaster of waiting or is this the disaster of not knowing what you are waiting to wait upon? This complete twisting of words while calculating which exchange of syntax, sentence structure and defining which arraignment is correct is getting under my skin. With all of this, why is it only getting under your skin?

Whenever purpose is unknown, the natural thing to do is to resort to all types of oxymoronic interpretive statements. This exemplifies the fact, that we are completely unaware, and uncertain of what to say or how to reply when moments of frustration last longer than expected. Such responses as; 'get on out of here, you're getting on my nerves' or 'you're giving me a headache' often show how ill-informed we are in matters of "Frustration Passage" and in matters of 'Frequent Frustration Resolution'.

As surreal as all of this is, are any of the solutions esteemed possible? The demand of purpose seems to make everyone cringe to think that those statements are possible. When we make such statements as 'stop it before you make a fool out of yourself, or stop it before I make a fool out of myself or stop it, you're making a fool out of me. Although each statement is probable. If such is done, with whose permission are they conducted? We all live in a world that seems to be more and more make believe. The more mature in age that we become it appears to only be make believe. With all of the opportunities given, can we afford to not make what only appears to be make believe, real? If that appeals to your individuality, do read further, we are only beginning.

Completing this page with peeked interest as to what transpires next is a great way for your curiosity to become engaged deeper. Certain statements should capture your attention. Not only should certain things captivate you attentively, but they are designed to peak your curiosity, while entertaining you permanently, and maintaining its original intent. Keeping your interest ongoing is only one degree of being able to continue effectively and efficiently. If your attention ever wanes, the difficulty of regaining the same level of interest is different. Each level of interest should have potential attached. It is almost as if there is some relevant reason that a person's attention is caught/captured. Certain subliminal suggestions (messages) are missed but the linguistics of the messages are caught as they are subtly designed for that intent. There is nothing that just happens. Everything that happens has a specific reason, reasoning and intentional design. If not, what is the reason for fishing? Fishing can be for provision or for fun but fishing has become a relaxation art as a sport.

Purpose, this variation of wording can be pronounced differently if the sentence structure deems the need for it. Before we discuss more indepth lets introduce words that are spelled the same but are different in meaning. Your reasons for reading are more my reasons for writing; a mutual need is met and they both are satisfactory.

The word 'purpose' has originality. It is somewhat impossible to continue throughout life without ever endeavoring upon 'originality or intent'. The two words are discussable terms being that they both establish some type of systemic systematic logic. The reasoning of frustrations logic is on a need to know basis. If you do not know the reasoning of frustration and why it is so often introduced in the spectrum of humanity our only result will be recidivism of an endless cycle continually associated with both anger, hostility and disappointment ending in the vicious cycle of blaming others for where you are or for what you have not accomplished.

An adequate choice of words in the sentence above all point towards one direction. Yes, you can be heard clearly as you internally ask yourself repeatedly this one selfsame question; why am I so 'frustrated'.

Before answering, lets attempt to define, locate, and to diagnose.

Purpose defined; is the original reason that a person is created. It is also the reason a thing is discovered and the immediate intent that an object is brought into existence, as by design. In life, there is no greater discomfort than not knowing your purpose personally or your reason for being alive. Every circumstance created, every situation that you are experiencing, have experienced or ever will experienced has a purpose. No circumstance, situation or experience is ever wasted. Ever human experience has an intent. There is an outcome, there is a purpose attached to every experience, associated with each event in life. The thing that needs realization first is the fact that, you are not "A Mistake". However, as I, I'm sure that you have made plenty of mistakes. But one thing is certain, "You Are Not a Mistake". Everything that you are and everything about you is unmistakable. Certainly, there are some things that are absolutely give and take based upon the faultiness of humanity in creation. However, otherwise everything is perfect. You are so much on purpose that you cannot be duplicated, copied you may or even cloned but you are the 'original'!

First, frustration is designed to remove you away from yourself, secondarily, it is assigned to remove you from your originality. ~ Chief Apostle M.III~

However, as this is attempted, frustration only brings you to your originality. Not only will you find yourself, you will discover vast discoveries personally as frustration forces you to deal with yourself while you are unearthing precious commodities within. The coal has a goal. The coal's goal is very insightful in its purpose. The coal with time as it is under pressure convert to a substance of substantial wealth. Coal has multiple uses. i.e. one of its many purposes can keep a home toasty and warm while keeping a family out of the cold by producing heat. What is it that your frustration has emotionally provoked you to discover? But you have not given yourself the openness to think outside of the emotions of hostility, instead, you're avenging yourself, you're taking revenge. Frustrations can take you away from your hostility, into tranquil moments where there is creativity as is designed, you will discover you are not as angry, bitter or even as cynical as you have portrayed.

The purpose of 'frustration' is to bring you to an awareness of your own individuality. However, you are afraid of self-discovery. There are frustrations which are only fears, fears which are used as permanent excuses. Each excuse which was relied upon is no longer accessible. Every excuse is now nonexistent and unavailable. Frustrations original assignment is negativity. Frustrations original assignment doesn't have to be fulfilled. Frustration's original negative intent cannot be fulfilled unless permission is provided. This permission must be provided by the person who is frustrated. Once an awareness of the intent of frustration is discovered with its destructive nature prior passivity can never be held dear to nor retained. The awareness concerning frustrations initial assignment completely changes your life. This awareness instantaneously places you in the drivers' seat. At this point, if a new direction is chosen, the new direction will be your choice completely. The fleeting feeling of being uncomfortable is necessary.

What is especially important is choosing to do something significant with the uncomfortableness you are experiencing. If you are comfortable angry, living lies and blaming others your medical bills will soar as will every opportunity in a negative direction. A marker determining the worth of everything is life is invisibly placed. Everything in life has this marked distinction. The value marker can be positive or the value marker can be negative and disposed as trash or unnecessary. It is truly up to you to correctly assess your worth. However, how each markers value is determined determines your choice of words and actions. There's no neutrality. You're either moving forward or you are moving further backwards.

Why does it appear that everything is so difficult, why does it appear that everything has to be one way or the other? What happened to everything being only black or white, why so many different colors to choose? Welcome to the real world. Excuses and spewing vitriol will not move you forward in the minutest terms. Just as you have a purpose and a purpose has an intent, and an intent has a possible reason for why things are carried out the way that they are, 'frustration' also has a purpose, an intent and a possible reason. The only difference is that 'frustration' takes often what is not chosen. What frustration takes is "opportunity"! Frustration does not have a concern as to who you are or even if you are able to endure. Frustration takes what it wants and afterwards, frustration takes over, and ooh walaa, personal embarrassment or crime scene. Experiencing aggravation, being distressed, excessive tiredness, anxiety, inopportune denials maritally; those consistent no's, headaches, backaches, insensitivity to the needs in a relationship all lead to differing perspectives of 'frustration'. If things continue as they are, all parties involved hurt, everything suffers needlessly. Symptomatically we can view the negative aspects of frustration have not only driven a deep wedge in the form of an un-crossable chasm but frustration is guaranteeing the security of its job with negative future benefits. As a rule, with our culture as a yard marker, many things that should cause hurtful responses are dismissed as normal, while you are told to get over it.

If you do not address peacefully the thing(s) that you are told to get over, you will never get over any of the things that you are unwilling to address. Anything unaddressed always gives life to multiple layers of undealt with 'frustration'. There is no life in this, only death! As can be noted frustrations demeanor can be convincing. When you are irritated like none other? If you are not aware of your actions the negative side of frustration(s) can complicate things more and will not give the comforting words or the emotional support that you need. The unfulfilled desires will haunt you so that you will almost forfeit what purpose you are aware of. This becomes an opportune assignment to further your indignant behavior. Whenever you have the opportunity, take the opportunity. Take the opportunity presented to deeply investigate within yourself, attentively, perceptively learning what appears to be a disadvantage is not always a disadvantage but places you at an advantage. We will approach next what will be the positive aspects of frustration in its unveiled presence of purpose. Prepare as we engage 'Purposes Promise'.

Purpose will always arrange and establish advantageous circumstances. Purpose also creates tailor-made circumstances dictated specifically for you. Purposes intent and its deliberation is staged and stacked in your favor for you to fulfill your 'purpose'. This setup or apparent hijacking as it may seem is associated with 'Purposes Promise'. The origin is easily deciphered. Here is a once in a lifetime deal, purpose makes a promise that can be fulfilled. Today begins an ordeal with 'purpose' in a positive manner. When a person is overcome by frustration they normally complicate issues but miss the miracle of its purpose. Purpose never reveals its hand until an inquiry is made. If no inquiry is ever made, purpose seems to only hide in the abyss of the soul never awakened. The awakening of purpose begins with a defiant act. A defiant act begins the awakening. What is the defiant act that awakens 'purpose'?

The defiant act that awakens 'Purpose' must also interchangeably involve 'Destiny's' awakening. Once awaken both arise simultaneously to assist the other. Circumstances awakens the slumbering 'Giants' with situations that are overwhelmingly to vast to surmount alone. The two begin their assault together as one! A third party also arises. The third parties name is 'Dreams'.

To reiterate that 'Purpose' is a live entity which navigates within, for some this would be outright heresy. However, this proposed heresy can withstand the force of everyone who would attempt to quell its truth; they would lose, unfortunately.

A truth that is overlooked is nonetheless still an overlooked truth until accepted, embraced and acknowledged.
~ Chief Apostle M.III ~

Where the roads within intersect is the internal hearts query and the soul's solstice. The fury for purpose begins and frustrations end. Such a soliloquy. The aftermath does not silence the quest for purpose. Purpose and its quest is only intensified yet refusing to be quieted. Everything you've longed for is present, presented, and accounted for. Your uniqueness is only masked by the degree of your frustration. Not only is your uniqueness masked it is masked with a plea. It is masked with a plea to be revealed to be unveiled. Such is unheard of in the same breath, so is the understanding. The understanding is steeped in vivid reality, but yet awaits an urgent appeal. To appeal or to not appeal, that is the question. How is it possible to remain in an indifferent behavior, condensed concisely with an attitude of rhetoric is an absolute quest for truth, although no statement is presented and not one question asked. It is yet a quest for "Purposes Promise".

Who has ever heard of such a thing; "Purposes Promise"?

Every individual has it written within. Their 'DNA' signifies such. As multiple questions begin their invasion swirling into the human mind, from within the human mind a phenomenon takes place. Questions arise like flowers thought to be dead, dormant thoughts arise like forgotten dreams of the night utterly taking every opportunity as they are triggered by some momentary event freshly remembered. Indelible impressions that were imprinted upon the soul now find an escape hatch. Completely amazing yet difficult to comprehend, this is what you accept as you acknowledge, there must be something greater, purposely fulfilling, and more adventurous. Your quest begins. Anonymous you can no longer remain. Something more prolific, something more profound has its grip, its gaping grasp upon you. It has your heart and soul as it strums a beat, a foreign tune, a sound of exchange. Your undivided attention is immediately wrapped without question in complete intrigue. It has happened to you and you are now attentive enough to actually give the attention necessary for what you are about to encounter. Every area of your life is in preparation for this invasion. The invasion of an ethereal substance that has lain dormant within. Hyperventilating, your breath shortens as though you are about to be thrust into another would be normal panic attack. You brace yourself for this as normal, it has become your comfort zone however, this time you are in for a lifelong surprise.

This is not your normal panic attack.

It is not an attack. It is an intuitive invasion from within. As a quest for knowledge has increased a visitor has been waiting. This visitor has been waiting for your curiosity to reach proportions unable to be taken control of by you or the others that have greater influence upon your life as your circle of peers, friends, acquaintances and alliances. This challenge is yours and yours alone.

The inquiry that you have has just granted permission to "General Purpose". A long awaited 'Five Star General', of life. This is your meet and greet ceremony as you are and have been inducted into the 'Army of Life'. Welcome to the world of "Purpose"! Purpose can never be denied of its intent. Frustration has awakened purpose. This is now the scenario. Hi, good day (morning, afternoon, evening, after night falls). I would like to thank you for awaking me. My name is 'Purpose'. I am 'Frustrations' arch enemy. I am 'Frustrations' arch nemesis. I am 'Frustrations' worst nightmare. I have been awakened to take you away from

"Frustrations" evil side. I am here to introduce you to 'Frustrations' good intentions for your life.

An awakening occurred through the questions of 'Why am I alive', 'What's my purpose', 'What am I doing here', and 'Why did I make it here (being born) alive'? Statements such as; why is this happening to me, why am I experiencing this, why can't I make it, why can't I get ahead in life, and why does everything have to be about them and not about me?

The fore stated are only some of the apparent questions that frustration presents from a negative position/perspective. This negative side of frustrations is designed to dummy you down to wear you out. It is designed to caused frequent negative self-esteem/self-worth problems. If you had no need for affirmation from others where would your life be? Having a need for healthy affirmation without the controlling behavior of those used to affirm is logical, credible and necessary. The unhealthy control, and the unnecessary dependence is the complication. No one is above, no one is beyond or below the need for healthy affirmation.

Currently, what is your greatest need?

Your greatest need has everything to do with you being affirmed personally. It is in the moment that affirmation appears to be the overdramatic need that we can find ourselves connecting to others who are truly unhealthy while the negative aspects of frustration seize us relentlessly contributing to our demise or death. Now your frustration is beyond your wildest dreams. Even your frustration has frustrations. This frustration comes with a complete inability to see. A view to perceive that your current frustrations are all the answers you have searched for most of your life. Now the answer presents itself in the form of every question that you have ever asked aloud or within.

What you have always desired is available. No longer are you having to wait in the long line of life furthering your frustration; Purpose is here "Now"! ~ Chief Apostle M.III

As we begin our long-awaited interview with "Purpose" there are a few things we must address to clear the air. The thing that happens next prevents progress. Our first encounter is to remove the blame game; removing the blame game takes place instantaneously most times once blame shifting is acknowledged or recognized. This first course of dialogue; where were you, why did you not come sooner, I needed your help. I've made too many mistakes, my experiences have been too vast, I have no need of 'you or your help, now'.

How can you help?

I hate you, leave me alone. The language of immaturity begins with un-forgiveness seething in unfathomable disgust.

This is spoken in every sentence. The words are so objectionable, so painful, as the heart aches with disappointment. Every evasive attempt does not cease as your initial response and interview begins. As each area of objectionable offense is addressed, an opening for your heart is given. The embittered battle that your mind has warred with can now begin to embrace the offers of "Purposes Promise". It is time, the presentation is made, now "Purpose" enters. The purpose of frustrations dialogue, the interview begins.

Hi, my name is "Purpose". It is good to finally meet you, I've been awaiting you and your inquiry. Your inquiry has awakened me intentionally. So, from this day forth prepare to live your life as intended. I have been activated and commissioned. My assignment is to literally assist you in the fulfilling of your assignment. Each part of our package deal is to positively revisit all your past, settle your present and to further fulfill all of your future frustration. Surprisingly, you attempted to awaken me years ago, but you were afraid! Frustration and I have fought over your questioning. It was negatively determined by frustration that I never awaken nor would I ever surface in a positive manner to be of any assistance to you, but through time, I 'Purpose' have prevailed to help you overcome, and not to overcome only, but to prevail successfully for the rest of your life.

Oftentimes during moments of your greatest distress,

unknowingly, without much thought being given, you began my awakening. The nights in which you spent alone outside gazing at the moon while watching the stars, an early mornings gaze at the beauty of a sunrise and after a long difficult day your heart would pitter-patter for the evening sunset while deeply peering off into the distance, the words would be uttered, what's the use, nothing seems to be going my way, nothing seems to be working or I just can't win for losing. Each moment that this occurred, I "Purpose" arose to assist, but as quickly as I arose, I was with more swiftness denied the opportunity to assist.

My (Purpose) knowing that I alone was the whom and the what you needed, every single time. But graciously I bowed out being that I was not welcomed and that you were not ready to receive the help that I would give or my personal innate assistance of which I would provide. Now at last, we are here like two stars crossing paths falling out of the galaxy into the earth's atmosphere being seen from afar. The speed provided for safe impact into the earths atmosphere is incalculable, the descent assigned while falling, first to prevent human casualties and you cascaded out of orbit directly onto and into me. Such was my privileged honor to provide safe passage for you to exist.

Again, allow me to reintroduce myself, my name is; "Purpose". I have safely and clearly prepared the way for you to 'live'.

Frustration (your very own) would have defeated 'you' eons

ago but because I had a reason to be, I fought for you so that you would awaken me, with your questions. I'm "Purpose" and I've always been. I watched your preparation. I quietly, silently slipped answers to you subtlely. As your grades rose higher others wondered at your progress. It was I, "Purpose", rising and falling at your very subconscious command. I peeked out to see if you were ok, to view the people that you were choosing to associate with. My choice for you would have been different, but I was asleep, put to sleep by 'you' multiple times.

I wish that I could have helped you before. But my help you silenced, silencing me, putting me back to sleep. I recall every wrong turn along the way with every wrong decision, I remember explicitly when things began to veer from the path originally planned and provided. The greatest thing that I (Purpose) remember are the 'Promises' that were made by you, that if you will or if I ever get out of this.

More importantly, I remember the 'Promises' made by 'Him (your Creator)' that if you ever begin to question while you're under great stress, duress or frustration that I (Purpose) was to avail myself, and to awaken to your rescue. Today here I (Purpose) am, availed and awakened to assist, to inform you of your next steps to be taken by you.

Awakened, availed and available to you, Purpose I am with 'Promises' galore guaranteed to succeed. Today, I (Purpose) will inform you as to the whys, the who's', the what's or any other lingering unanswered questions. I (Purpose) make no mistakes, in everything that I do I complete and fulfill. The awareness of passion, beginning with frustration is not only a "purpose" but you are possessing "Purpose". You are "Purposeful" your purpose is 'crystal clear' without negativity.

I (Purpose) have watched you struggle with frustration. The struggle you've had with frustration has been the ensuing battle which has left you constantly at the mercy of defeat. Today, your marching orders change, you will begin to march at the beat of a different sound.

As you give your case to 'purpose', and your cause an all-out battle begins for frustrations complete subjugation. People should not be subjugated, but frustration is not a person, it is an emotion. Frustration is a possibility. If frustration is properly deployed while being employed correctly, frustration brings about lasting sustainability, profiting with "Purpose". So, fear not; "Purpose" is here!

Most individuals in their perspective would only view purpose as "a mission. The mission of what am I here for? Many obstacles can be built upon with this line of thought rationalization. The thought in and of itself is not wrong. However, if we are willing to leave the restrictions/confinements while stepping away from thoughts that limit. A better position of thought is "Who am I here for"? The distress that comes with 'what am I here for' can cause an internal imbalance to become very disheartening and equally disorienting. Overwhelming streams of frustration become self-intoxicating when excluding others that are presently more frustrated than you. Too often we see people as opportunities and not opportunities as people. Could it be that I am here for you and my fulfillment comes because of seeing you complete your designed intent (Purpose). The intent for which you are created instead o~

The quote above establishes the human perception of cognitive thought described as cognition, cognitive thought perception based upon actions taken while thinking. It is the complete inability to function for certain individuals while under conscious thought. This is often displaced by/with subconscious thought(s) with actions thereby creating 'frustration and frustrations' momentum.

If this momentum is capitalized upon its nexus is "Purpose" alliterated. At each point, we find purpose. Once purpose is found, it is possible to extract the intent and purposes reason for being and existing in every case. It is the most common thing imaginable. Frustrations purpose to disorient is a normal action only if you are overwhelmed.

The thinker thinks. Without thoroughly thinking a misfiring of thoughts takes precedent. Thoughts, that are not properly thought through or processed adequately in order for presentation to others. Onlookers only gaze hypnotically at those who are thinkers admiring them until the thinker stops thinking and behaves rashly in frustration. Such necessity should model thought(s), frustration only begins within if there is originality in need of being created. You only become frustrated if there is a project to complete which has not been recognized within. You will never fail if you choose to cooperate with such "Creative Frustration"; begin and complete!

Frustration properly harnessed creates "energy", "Creative Energy". If frustration is not properly harnessed, it can become one of the deadliest emotions thereby corrupting the human essence through total disruption. This disruption is known as 'unacknowledged purpose'. ~ Chief Apostle M.III~

Frustration is a methodology that will never go away. Even in peaceful times it is designed as the fuel for authentic fire even in discussions of philosophy. Once a person is infused with frustration, an ongoing pursuit overtakes as they search for ways to put out this fire. An antidote for frustration is the medication of "Purpose". With each step taken, you will find the fires of frustration. If frustration is present, so is purpose; frustrations ability awakens along with its creative content. Question each situation before, now literally pursue until you quiet frustrations passion. This is to be involved with "Purpose"!

An involvement that has no quarantine is to be based upon unsubstantiated thought without a premise. Things that are not drawn out find no purpose. Once purpose is relented, a thorough examination should be conducted as to why there is no pursuit to fulfill what passion has presented or is designed to produce. Being in a stage of noncompliance will forever complicate every level of success. It is not possible to produce or to promote what you are not willing to passionately pursue. Having the proper view and innately allowing what is already fulfilled, completed to manifest is what your whole prioritization should include, nothing should include the nod for passivity, only passion.

Every phase of life comes with instructions. If the instructions for the phase of life that you are currently experiencing are not continually followed properly a deficit is created. Each phase of life has its own intentionality attached. The manual should be addressed and follow accordingly, the manual for life does not need a rewrite nor does the same manual need the interpretation for or from someone who does not have your life skills of your life specifications. What works for you, in every other word under the sun very well may not remotely work for them. It is important to schedule constant schedules with yourself.

These are appointments that you must keep, it is impossible to cancel appointments with yourself!

At no time present or at any time future or in between will you ever be without you, yourself, your me, myself and I. Get used to it, use for your good and benefit substantially from it; you are always there.

POWER IN THE PRESSURE COOKER FRUSTRATION

CHAPTER 5

EXPECTANCY

The extreme value of everything in life is based upon expectancy. If you have no expectations, frustrations will never have any merit whatsoever in your life.

What are your expectations? Everyone, everywhere has them!

Everyone has expectations. If the expectations that others have are never mentioned does it deny the fact that expectations preexisted. If something or someone doesn't meet your expected standards there will manifest a level of disappointment although the degree of disappointment remains hidden. Greater disappointments are experienced when promises are made but promises are not kept. This furthers frustration. This type of frustration also creates static and tension between individuals if the expectations made from promises do not bring about whatever was desired. Possibly, the intuitive thoughts are maybe I should never expect anything from anything or anyone being that nothing is ever followed through when promised. What you are experiencing is something that everyone experiences when promises are made, never kept, only delayed. Distrust begins, ill-tempered actions manifest while individuals explode in fits/tirades, and a host of other things begin. Maybe, just maybe your acts/actions are justifiable but the underlying actions are caused by constant expectations over time never being fulfilled. Just empty promises. Yes, everyone that I know gets tired of them also; and no one is exempt with the very same expressions of, it is enough!

So, what do I do?

Well, I'm glad that someone was brave enough to ask, to admit and to seek counsel, to seek help without continuing to suppress just how hostile or frustrated they are. It is unbelievable the number of people who withhold how internally angered they are. They put on the same face morning by morning, day by day portraying a lie. Frustration isn't to be hidden nor was it ever meant to hide. It is important that frustration be expressed calmly, rationally and discretely otherwise volatile issues that are more candid take place. In the current culture suppression of frustration is how most handle how their feelings are expressed. Not giving a care does not cease the way you feel. Your feelings are only intensified and your level of frustration and response becomes deeply callous. If you've paid attention to a callous, the additional layer of hardened skin stops sensitivity. Being insensitive may cost you something gorgeous or it may cost you something beautiful that can never be replaced. Something replaced does not have the same sentiment or value as what is/what was the original. It is ridiculously impossible to go around ordering everyone to pick up the pieces. What are you willing to afford yourself so that your frustrations become applications that are approved and appreciations of everything that you have ever desired?

Your expectancy is a forecast. Expectancy is not a dilemma.

An entered dilemma is when you have no expectation for anything or of anyone. The only thing learned is to walk around critically frustrated because of your very own cynicism.

Who have I become?

This question for some would be stated best if there were supportive groundwork.

So, who have you become?

This is the reply most intellectuals retort.

Who have you become based upon the level of your

frustration is this writer reply?

Remember, another form of frustration, is hostility. Hostility is deeply rooted anger laced with rhetorical sarcasm. Nothing, and no one is good enough. Everything is insufficient for this type of character. Their nature is destructive, and volatile. This ridiculous nut is 'Bruce Lee's dead nemesis nuanced with 'Fists of Fury', subject to just punch and to hit you repeatedly. Their only reason, is to see if punishment can be inflicted, watching you grimace in pain physically, while adapting to the pain emotionally.

Such behavior should never be solicited or endorsed nor kept quiet but should be reported immediately. Sure, you are frustrated, but it is not right for you to take your frustration out on those you do not know nor on the ones that you do know and profess to love or that love you in return. The dangers of frustration are the unscheduled moments of emotional outbursts that not only is spoken vehemently but actions ensue as though something or someone else has taken control of you. Moment, when you cuss without warning and for no sufficient reason, you just become belligerent with ready rapidity. Reasons given, I'm frustrated. In the way that this is handled is very juvenile. It is as though; the whole world owes you something. Somehow, you've forgotten that we are all contributors or maybe that was never told you. You were not informed.

What has taken place?

Uninformed people go through ritual. The uninformed do things as though they know exactly what they are doing. But the uniformed by doing so cause great harm. Not only do they cause great harm to themselves but their ritual causes harm to others, making things bad/difficult for everyone. Rituals are often performances. The performance of a ritual is most often performed to get attention. The attention often desired is for approval. If the approval or the nod of approval is not received it can contribute to further frustration. The level of frustration that this affords. The term affords is used often. A reason for the term afford being used often is due to the expense and the great elevated lengths that we go to receive approval. That/this is the human factor is all people with no reference to skin color. Individuals change based upon acceptance or rejection. This effect is upon everyone. Does this appear to put you in the dark? If so we all have been there, some have been in the dark longer than others. Nonetheless, everyone has been in the dark (in total ignorance performing rituals). We have been totally uncertain as to what we're doing. The normal pattern is to either follow the leader or to play as though we are leading and by default become the leader. This is the what as in our question above; what has taken place.

Everything works differently for different people. The same thing does not work for everyone. Frustration levels increase if you're attempting to be someone other than who you are. This is not advocating for deviance or immorality. More specifically this is directed in the path of frustration/what to expect. Everyone emulates someone at some point, but remember, you are unique, not a clone. The important thing is that we find our very own individuality. As we find our personal individuality it should emanate as a bright red moral compass establishing our resolve, our point of revolution, and the resolution of our frustration. This should work!

What have I become?

A person with integrity will need to answer the forthcoming question. Once we quell the difficulty of having to admit that we all, 'become'. The question we must answer is; what is it that we all become?

What have I become after I was born and now even later in life?

The prevailing truth is, what have I become?

If what I have become needs to be addressed and dealt with sternly, am I willing to sternly address ad to deal with it, in order to create the proper life discipline to catapult me into the place scheduled. Why does ending it all need to be the place?

This seems all too rhetorical.

Being conscious of what you have or have not become is often a demon's greatest nightmare. ~Chief Apostle M.III~

We've been afforded greater. Most certainly death is not to be welcomed. Death is not a friend, death is an enemy. Anything that we're entrusted with while we're alive should be focused upon as a task worthwhile and an accomplishment(s) worth completing. A wounded individual portrays animalistic instincts. Their only consideration is survival, nothing and no one else is important. Nothing otherwise matters.

The dangers of not properly healing become more noticeable when prematurely involving others. So, maybe, you have made the decision to not allow yourself the proper or necessary time to recover from everything that has happened. This does not resolve the fact that you are now angrier and more frustrated than you were before neither does it remove your hostility. When the opportunity is given to reconsider everything, at some point, life appears to become more puzzled, and people appear to become more perplexed. This is a grueling reality after considering the number of people year after year who are hurting, and others who are constantly hurting daily.

Does this present a problem?

Can you imagine what their feelings of hurt is turning/changing them into?

Certainly, the gender identity crisis stems from people who are in crisis mode without the proper outlet, we are assured. The loss of masculinity among men, the same exact loss of femininity among women is of grave consequence, and cause for reasonable concern.

This does not rule out certain proclivities humans lean toward from birth. They are habitual tendencies. A constant barrage of frustration can cause you to become insensitive.

Being that you have found yourself becoming who or what you are not, great insight is needed to assure that frustration is directed properly, not at things or the people that you love. A correct assessment of directing your frustrations towards your creative nature, and creativity that you hide so well encapsulated deeply within.

There is no further need for depression; "Create"!

An old remedy can cure all ills, or so we believed. ~ Chief Apostle M.III~

In a time when our fore parents used unrecognized, and possibly medically unapproved herbal concoctions for scrapes, cuts and bruises designed to soothe away the pain or to assist with a sprain while recovering from an injury. In the world of commercial advertisements, 'Cheerios' brand cereal states, 'kid tested, mother approved' but it only worked for kids until we became 'grownup kids'. We allowed mothers, fathers, uncles and aunts to experiment because grandma said or grandpa used products that stunk to high heaven, but they swore to the moon and back that they worked. If you have great grandparents who are alive or even grandparents, maybe what you have are only just the memories of those great moments. I'm certain that you have that gleam in your eye or you chuckled at the thought. Especially if the memories are healthy you missed them like mad crazy. You have probably been rescued multiple times by your grandparents from swats to your derriere or maybe they swatted your bum themselves. For some of you they may have protected you from getting your cane raised or getting your butt torn down or tore up. Whatever description befitting would probably be based upon what part of the country or world you reside.

The complete trust you showed or maybe did not show as they administered their own failsafe products to you if you were not well. The products were sworn to be a cure all.

Certainly, immediate relief was certain. Well, possibly at least, it was expected. One thing for sure, you knew the smell of vapor rub, whether it was "Vicks Salve/Vapor Rub" or a different unpopular product. It was sure that no one missed you or the smell as you walked or ran passed.

Turpentine was another product used for medicinal reasons.

Ah ha, what about the proverbial clothes keeper, known as "Moth Balls"? As you reached into the closet or the packed away clothing in the clothing storage trunk, once you were dressed, you as well as your clothing smelled like 'moth balls'! Uggggh, whew, it was expected. Once the moth balls were in place, the moth balls were to dispel rodents, moths and other insects that seemed to invade the closets like a hostile takeover without consent. The proposed insects and rodents seemed to penetrate even the securest areas. They were living in large luggage compartments known as clothing or storage trunks even in the luggage bags set aside for travel. For those who remember, those were the days. Now those days of yester yore are no more.

Today our lives are lived in a microcosm out loud, unmistakable, incapable of being missed. So now you ask, what happened to yesterday? Let's attempt to answer. Many people are asking.

What happened to yesterday, it became today! Yesterday, is {No longer available}. ~ Chief Apostle M.III~

Multitudes all over the world are attempting to live today with yesterday's mentality. As you probably have finally come to terms with, this is "Impossible". Each day carries its own ideas, mindsets and contemplations. So, should you.

You should not greet the day; the day should greet you welcoming your arrival. No aggravation, no frustration. Each day should be a celebration of you and your arrival. Today was awaiting you expecting your arrival. So, will "Tomorrow"!

However, are you ready or are you as excited and anticipative as tomorrow is about you being in it? That very moment when you realize that what you've been hoping and believing for while awaiting your miracle and "God's" miraculous intervention 'are' all tied to your "Frustration" ... The very same "Frustration" you have tried inadvertently to avoid; you are experiencing/have experienced! {Can somebody please say "Prestidigitation"}?! Many individuals are attempting to live out today with the mindset and the expectations of yesterday, last week, two months ago or even years ago. Your day to day mindset should not be the same. Becoming a hostage is what happens when there is no change in thinking/mindset. A mindset only remains the same if there is no growth or change. Maturity both escalates and elevates the minds set pattern, patterns and behaviors. If there are not alterations in patterns of/for thought the thinking/mindset causes hindrances which restrain successfulness in all areas.

In life, there must be growth; Growth in thought and growth in logic. No exceptions!

In a desperate dash of obscurity, hoping that someone you're attempting to avoid does not recognize you, you accidentally literally run smack dad into them. Obviously, you're shocked, your eyes meet, no words are exchanged nor are any words expressed. Nothing could ever be more awkward. Truly that was not expected, but it's so humorous. As you walk away after getting yourself up off the floor it takes you a moment to regroup. That was hilarious. As you attempt to regain your composure you humor yourself as you chuckle, giggling within. Now you're asking yourself, how'd that happen. Never in a thousand years would that incident have ever been imagined. There were no expectations of this ever-taking place, but it has. Was it planned by either of you? No, it was not planned by you or the other person, yet it happened. Did time or fate foresee this taking place? Was it set up for the two of you to intersect your lives on that date or day?

We may attempt to explain this away as fate or chance. This was not just a random possibility. To tie a bow or to tie a shoestring, the strings must cross or so we were taught earlier in life. Something similar takes place even in the accidental tying of tying a knot in a shoelace. The ropes, the strings, the cords are set to produce what is necessary for safely. The appeal engaged in eventful, intentional, interactive tying for the purpose intended. Although the mechanisms used have no human emotions attached nonetheless they are engaged for the purpose(s) intended. If any of the above mechanisms were emotional would they object?

This is a question to be pondered over from deep within without the answer being surfaced or superficial.

CHAPTER 6

LIVE

"Now"; this, is where you get the opportunity to live. This should not be misunderstood and taken as 'when' you get the opportunity, but 'where' you get the opportunity to 'Live'. The presentation of life also presents the opportunity to "Live". Everything that has breath and that is born alive has the opportunity to live. How you choose to live is somewhat of a different story. An opportunity presented as a 'when' determines time, a set time. Equally so an opportunity that is presented as a 'where' determines a set location. Being constantly frustrated will consistently force you to miss two of the most important pieces of information necessary for you to "Live" and to "Live out Loud" intentionally!

It is so therapeutic to begin. Life awaits you.

Are you ready?

The discipline that it takes to begin is just that, discipline, it is a discipline awaiting you and your willing participation. Nothing is as difficult as presented, the complications major from the minor frustrations that you have believed, accepting as being true. Taking a stiff drink during this time of the day will not put the frustrations of the heart that you've experienced away, they will only compound what you already know. Drinking and driving are a self-induced vertigo deluding your judgement. Certainly, you are not aware of how this although it appears that your equilibrium is off. Maybe you have dedicated your life to a whole lot of worry and living has never been in the equation. But living has always presented itself. The truth factor is other than what has appeared; living has been unacknowledged. For too long, living has not been an accepted module. Living has only been an option. As unknown as this truth is it has yet to be accepted.

A life worth truly living involves you.

No truer statement can be made of life other than the details of, it takes you to 'Live' it. When thinking in terms of defining the word "Live" it also interchanges with the word 'Live. The word 'Live' correlates with the word 'Life'.

The first word, which is the word, 'live', correlates with something that is living, breathing and alive. The second word which is spelled 'live' refers to something in the presence of, in which you are an audience. i.e. such as a performance or an audition. Both words are synonymous, the two words are spelled the same in their spelling and each word must have the ability to connect with 'Life' at any point. Possibly, the similar spelling is contradicting to most. The fact that you are alive while life is presently passing them by is conflicting at best. It is the fact of not knowing how to capture the life that they most desire to live stirs the inner frustration that is most likely displayed, assuredly is fear. I'm certain that most people become delusional or paranoid when they hear the words from someone that they love to 'Go Get a Life'. Even if it the words are from someone who means well; the moment that the words "Go Get a Life" are spoken, just as quickly as the words were spoken, frustration and panic surface. Frustration and panic set in and in no uncertain terms, so does fear. Surely, there are reasons that this frequent show stopping line up of 'frustration, panic and fear' announces its arrival. Their arrival is announced with a vengeful, show stopping vendetta. If you are more matured in years, it is certain that you have attempted to solve this mystery as you look back over your life analyzing certain events. There's this unknown factor of why did I not take the initiative to do that. Anytime you're attempting to finalize memories as to what your 'that' was or is becomes increasingly disturbing. Having more possibilities is an unsettling reality as you face the days that your life has not been lived the way that you earnestly desired your life to be lived. Now in life, everyone is collaborating with a financial analyst or an estate planner, a hospice care worker, hospital while finding referrals to senior citizens homes or something otherwise. There is a problem with this, it is not your ideal. The disturbing thing that you now realize, is that you opted out of 'Life', you did not 'Live'. The three humorous onstage showstoppers seem more present than ever. No, it's not 'Larry, Curly or Moe' as humorous as the 'Three Stooges' are.

It's those other three guys, "Frustration, Panic and Fear".

Their arrival is not unannounced.

You were introduced to all three. Queasy was your inner name for years, most of your life. One thing is certain, this keeps everyone on equal terms. These three guys (Panic, Frustration and Fear) are always remembered. Every person on the planet has experienced their attempted takeover. The attempt to be held hostage in your own human unit, within you.

As an example, the crossing of a large body of water. When crossing such a large body of water, it must be strategically conducted. The plans must be strategic to be executed safely. Everyone involved should be completely compliant with what is being undertaken. Every person who has agreed to take the trip has entrusted their lives to the systematic planning strategy of those in charge. This is quite a undertaking and the responsibility is huge. In the crossing of the bridge, no ship or boat is included. There are no watercrafts. It is a 'Bridge'! No prior experience or experimentation established a precedent for this venture. This adventurous advent will surely be eventful as scheduled, with all hands on 'deck'. Undertakings of this magnitude take great solitude and perception. When human lives are involved there is nothing riskier. Nerves will be frazzled with possible tempers flaring knowing the reality of what is at stake. The weightier matter is who is at stake. This processing can be overtaxing. The process can be overwhelming, while delaying the obvious. If the undertaking or the project is considered a go, once the go is successfully conducted, the belief that each person as a strategist increases as does their credibility with others. The lending institutions will now go above and beyond to finance success.

Does this present the persons involved as though they were not successes before this undertaking was recognized as successful?

Was this necessary to catapult those who succeeded to create personal recognition or was this the need of others? Was this for the onlookers, the lending institutions/the underwriters who would capitalize off their success in order to be catapulted into verifiable status?

Remember, your success will also effectively help others catapult. Success always causes you to launch successfully. The experience of success has the domino effect. Each level of your success inspires others. Personal success should not be a onetime event. ~ Chief Apostle M.III~

The last quote is the drumroll to begin 'Life'; this drumroll is your cue to 'Live'! With perched anticipation, the cue of when to begin has anxiously been awaited. All over the world everyone waits for that special moment, this is your cue; "Live". Whatever resonates, this sound does not imply immorality. "Live"! Live like there is no tomorrow. Make this day your 'Best'. Begin things that you were afraid to do before this moment. This does not imply lawlessness. Take a disciplined position of not only beginning, but completing the things which you have started. Watching others soar, cheering them on is admirable, but what about you.

Admiring others only appearing to fly as you ponder how, only to realize they have never left the ground. This is very disappointing if only to realize that you have been envious of a grounded bird with broken or clipped wings. What appeared to be flight was a delusional myopic illusion. The illusion of grandstanding and mirages. The illusion of an innate desert mentality gone psychotic. If you choose to accept the fact that no one can soar, soaring will never be your forte. There's no reason to sit back and wait for others.

The person learns to soar can instruct others how to soar. If we would only take a moment we can glean valuable insight from those who have succeeded in expertise that we are pursuing.

Soar! Do not wait for someone other than yourself to soar. Do not watch others take to the runway in flight when you are the initial paradigm setter and paradigm shifter; Shift and Soar! ~ Chief Apostle M.III~

Just when you thought that the 'Phoenix' had landed you find yourself soaring. No, this time it is not imaginative. It is shocking isn't it. Without thought, no pretentiousness or hesitation, you are not on the runway taxiing awaiting permission to take off, but you're soaring. It is mind boggling how quickly a scenario changes.

Moments ago, you were paranoid, delusional, almost losing it. If you soar without thought, a perfect lesson is missed. No soaring takes place if the laws that reinforce soaring are not recognized. There are certain laws that surround the activity of soaring although they are not consciously acknowledged. Soaring has rules set in place to soar. Once the participants meet the requirements soaring begins. The soaring program in life continues providing lessons. Some are accepted, others, are not accepted but refused. Refusing certain lessons does not dismiss nor rid us of the subject matter or lessons. The subject matter, and the lessons only show up to be faced at a different time in life. Study, thereby learning the lessons well, take the test now so that later in life, no lessons and no test surface untaken. If lessons are refused and dismissed they show up later in life at a more inopportune time. The inconvenience of lessons presented but refused make life very uncomfortable.

Lessons of great importance are the lessons of being completely totally alert and having your undivided attention. Others can afford to not pay attention, but you are different. For you, complete alertness is very important; you cannot afford distractions.

Distractions costs! Distractions price is too expensive. The price for distractions are way overrated. Distractions are another form of 'suicide'. ~ Chief Apostle M.III~

Consider this, a quick glance in the wrong direction. What's the price, where will this quick glance place you?

If this quick glance is taken while driving, countless lives can be lost in a split second. If it is a business deal, once you become distracted even for a moment could be the difference in securing or losing a business deal or losing the business contract. One thing that I'm quick to note among those who are in business while creating business deals/business contracts is the knack to recognize who's really interested or who's not interested by their lack of attentiveness. Certain undisciplined acts or actions should not become the cause of not securing the contract/deal. Dealing with individuals in business is serious and risky.

The perceptions of business people who are all business is

different. Fortunately, life affords the position to 'Live' even while busily engaged in business. Is there a no-go zone in business? Perhaps this no-go zone in business is only recognized or known by the individuals that have been in business long enough to understand the code language established among business elitists. They have acquired the knowledge of where this invisible no-go zone exists.

If there are unknown invisible zones you will quickly learn every zone.

"Basic instructions before leaving earth" is the ascribed meaning which defines the acronyms used for the word 'Bible'. A major portion of all of life has been derived from that "Basic instructions before leaving earth" book known as the 'Bible'. It is the instruction manual that teaches how to 'Live'. Not only does this book give instructions of how to live but it also gives perfect instructions of what to do to get life to work for you. It is the corner cut man's solution. A boxing corners' cut man becomes greatly alarmed when the opponent has injured the title holder. The corners' cut man closely watches the fight as the defending champion defends the title.

The main focus of contending in the ring is not winning, it is 'living' to fight and defend the title. Some of the thoughts which enter the mind of a fighter would be humorous if they were shared. In the ring, the fighter portrays an image tougher than life. This tougher than life image portrayed is praying that you make it out of the fight 'alive'. Winning, yes. Winning and leaving the ring payed with every perk, including worldwide recognition, and lucrative endorsements. This is motivation enough to motivate you to fight and to win. Your face is known and recognized globally, your bruises and even your facial scars. Everyone watching see's you swollen and broken, but more evidently seen is your bruised ego. At the very moment that your hands are raised as the victor, your physical appearance appears as if you were defeated. What a fight!

Victory truly has been experienced. The price of victory has cost, you've paid to win. Assuredly you have the sweet rewards and the satisfaction of your labor. You look the part, face and all, definitely, you're not the underdog. The place of seamless victories has catapulted you to the forefront without question. Sweat less victory they say. The statement of sweat less victory almost lends to desperation. There is great possibility of achieving sweat less victory if great planning is at the forefront while preparation takes place. An important signpost to reflect upon is being able to recognize that this is one of your greatest milestones accomplished to date as you're preparing to 'Live'. Living does include your ability to plan well while also realizing that living becomes very competitive market. Knowing what you want in life helps and knowing the life that you have planned to live are important tools promoting progress. If you're not certain of what you want in life or if you're not sure of the life you have planned, life becomes hard, living becomes boring, mundane, disappointing and depressing.

Does anyone remember what you always desired to be when you were an impressionable small child?

The world was your stage and you would perform at the drop of a hat. The world is yet your stage, never forget.

What happened to those days?

Why are you so afraid of becoming what you've always desired?

Let's stimulate the desires of innocence. Let's stimulate your first glance of what you knew, and what you desired to become and to accomplish passionately.

Do you remember how brave you were when you wanted to be a 'Firetruck'?

Every bell and every whistle you provided alone. Running throughout the house or the neighborhood sounding like a firetruck on the way to put out your imaginary fire. Everyone laughed, but you imagined yourself as both the firetruck and the firefighter. Most of you remember the moment that you desired to be the nurse or the doctor, others desired to become a schoolteacher, the principal, a minister, the banker, a lawyer, the mad scientist, but sane as well, and on and on. The amazing thing is some of you were more than in puppy love you actually loved, believed that you would marry a certain person, you knew the number of children that you would have, you were assured of the social status that you desired for your family in the community you had envisioned that you would live as well as the place of your future employment.

What has caused your envisioned lifestyle to appear to have been lost in your childhood?

In fact, there are so many choices. The choices are so obvious, when it comes to life many are overwhelmed and fear choosing a career field, life or lifestyle. What is comforting and comfortable to you may not even appeal to the next person no not even remotely. This is how unique we are. Our seeming diversities at times over simplify and complicate things. No one is your clone. Even your supposed cronies don't desire to be you, even on your best day.

Suppose there is a substitute for life. My God, hopefully the substitute is not living. For some this substitute appears to be just that. No 'carpe diem'. It is like most are really running from the day and not seizing it. Opportunities galore await being embraced while multitudes await opportunity. It is almost a contradiction as opportunities await seizing and others cry for the opportunities that await. They find themselves in direct opposition. The opportunity and the individual. What if someone just decided to take all of the opportunities and place them in your home? However, in order to seize the opportunities, you are responsible for getting everyone to come out of your home lavatory, would you? In the lavatory is where most people get the most of their ideas.

Ideas are not aligned with oppositions. Ideas are lined with opportunities. If taken, ideas are being interwoven with opportunities, the advancements have no limitations. ~ Chief Apostle M.III~

The difficulty presents itself as the fear of opportunities. If opportunities to live are feared there are other realities which exist that are more destructive. No one dies from living too much. But living too much is what is feared the most; it is what we fear. In some nice way, we shut the ability to live down so as to await out our moment to die but having never lived. The fears that you fear are more afraid of you than you are of your fears. The fears that you fear, fear that you will live. In order for what you fear to take over you must nurture the fears that you fear. When you decide to 'live' also decide that no fear of living is granted permission to cease your ability/your choice you have chosen to live.

It really is not as dire or as difficult as it has been presented.

Advancement begins with you.

While you're awaiting the opportunity to get ahead and to begin your life, someone has taken the occasion you've chosen not to take. Any step forward is not a step that someone should take for you. The steps forward should be taken by you and by you alone. Once the confidence that was missing in your life is achieved, accepted, received and embraced you're enabled with unstoppable fortitude. The only thing that has held you back has been the fear of embracing the opportunities presented to you.

There is a source of mobility that you must accept. Once accepted, mobility creates an active way of activity, being immobile or being immobilized does not stand a chance. The sources of mobility are acceptance and responsibility. Acceptance and responsibility is the fuel for where you desire to be and to also remove yourself from where you are. It is not possible to be in two places at once.

It must be determined that if you are not here (the place that you are assigned to be) you are there (the place and the life that you are not assigned to live). The only thing that it takes to exist while forfeiting living is to assess where you are and become comfortable. In any moment that your comfort level outweighs your drive to succeed or to be successful dangerous waters are being treaded.

Forget the outbreak of formulated societal dilemmas based upon certain cultural proclivities that everyone is prone to repeat. Certain stigmas such as being born the wrong color or being born on the wrong side of the tracks are just that, stigmas but are not the ultimate rule of thumb. This is a time that we are concurrent with and it should be used to dismiss such enigmas that have been used to rule over others based upon color, societal skills and geography. It does not matter what term is used to recognize you, you are not the terminology or the euphemism projected.

The need to sing the Civil Rights song of 'we shall overcome' is in direct opposition of all that has been accomplished. There are many who have chosen to not overcome. Those who have chosen to not overcome are living under the stigma of another person's perceptive ideology but the choice they have chosen is theirs not yours. Again, no one needs to clone you or your decision no not even the cronies that you have embraced as your closest friends. The only necessity is that you begin to take notice of the 'Power' that is in your 'Pressure Cooker' for success!

POWER IN THE
PRESSURE COOKER
FRUSTRATION

CHAPTER 7

STEPS

Before beginning movement, profundity must strike with questions that boggle the human speculative.

When ordering my steps, how proficient should I be?

Should I be lenient, careless and reckless or should the profundity of my steps leave all of those that watch my gate (stride) gasping for air?

Perhaps they should be bewildered as I step into things that others have feared and failed to engage!

The thoughts that come to mind are unknown territory with

undetermined advancement. Unknown territory and undetermined advancement can cause speculation also leaving the stepper contrasting in deep speculation. Oh, but the rewards of moving humanity into oblivion due to the darkness. The unforeseen steps of advancement are foreboding. As exciting as this is, it can also lose its thrill if you are not the one spearheading the steps being taken. More questions begin to surface. However, the questions which begin to surface are not minutely in contradiction of the obvious advancements. The questions asked are from humans who are concerned. The individuals who ask are sane and normal. Their questions which were asked originated from deep within searching for answers. The questions posed stand, needing clarity, wise counsel and proper guidance as each question is correctly sufficiently answered. At any juncture where uncertainty resides, deep deliberation within always appears to crash the party. No celebration ever takes place if uncertainty is the ruling notion.

Nobilities need is to marry the steps in the direction(s) being taken. The merger of marrying your steps within this direction secures your arrival while divorce proofing both your purpose and your plans successfully.

Once you have united the necessary momentum in a collaborative effort, not only do you become a force to reckon with, you become 'unstoppable'. ~ Chief Apostle M.III~

Unstoppable forces are a threat to those who use objectives objectively but do not merge or marry their overall objectives. To not stagnate what is most important, the need to continue stepping is more important. Great moments will always create the force to propel and hurl you into an unknown place awaiting your decision(s) and command(s).

Success takes ultimatums, not suggestions! Whenever suggestions are given to success, success is assured that you are not sure of the potential of success. Successes degrees and the depths of success are always awaiting your command demandingly. ~ Chief Apostle M.III~

Nothing was, is or will ever be created without your being assured of what you desire, what you want, and what you are commanding to manifest.

Stop the presses, prepare yourself as you read the next statement. Greatness presses upon each of us. What greatness presses upon everyone with is this superimposing need.

This superimposing need for everyone is to be in complete total collaboration with what you have determined.

This is the greatest tool of 'Success'.

Hesitating to step or to take steps is the surest way to not see anything accomplished. The need to address is also the need to undress. Undress what appears as if it is the thing that you have breathed out or breathed forth as it masquerades before you but does not contain the commanded sustenance and substance. Take a moment to reflect upon what in life you have accepted, you're now immediately discovering that your sustenance and substance are not contained within. Many things are reflected upon but reflecting upon does not mean that you possess. Settling has become an 'art'! Once the art of settling takes place, you are no longer in charge.

The realization that the contents that you were anticipating are neither in the package or the container which holds the contents. Be certain to read everything before you agreeably sign your signature to the applicable line. Remember, some things are non-refundable others are non-returnable. Once the purchases have been made, they are yours. Awaiting things that have no substance or sustenance are 'Frustration' seekers. Be very practical about what you do, if not, you will find that the power seems to diminish if you are going forward.

Gratitude is a practiced art.

Stepping forward with a heart of creativity while possessing eager anticipation including thankfulness does wonders relieving pressure and removing pain.

A pressure cooker can become a deadly dangerous weapon if used improperly.

The pressure cooker is designed to be used as a safe and

more efficient way for food preparation. Foods that are safe for use in the pressure cooker and that are nutritionally edible are recommended and normally listed. Not following the manufactures specifications for use may be fatal. Knowing that we (human beings) attempt to be experimental with things that have labels for safety is a manufacturers worst nightmare. The safety precautions for the product have been placed for easy viewability although the directions and the instructions safely placed doesn't stop those who are given to curiosity.

Every year fatalities occur and are encountered by those who have chosen to avoid following the instructions provided for the specific use of certain products. Individuals find themselves in emergency rooms or without shelter as their possessions go up in flames; Inflamed, is an understatement. Contained force, power and restraint is displayed while the pressure cooker is in use. The constant steam being released is vital along with the whistling sound of power under pressure. The edible arranged meal is anticipated gleefully once the programmed time for the pressure cooker completes its task.

The mouthwatering, savory, edible, goodies which reside within, is power that is positive; napkins please!

There's never a negative perception or a negative illusion envisioned as the pressure cooker carries out its manufactured specifics. The moment of disapproval may take place, but it only takes place if you're famished and hungrier than the wait time given for the pressure cooker to complete the meal. Otherwise, we wait with bated anticipation for the meal without complaining. The aroma whiffs through as it intensifies anticipation for consuming. No one screams nor does sarcasm towards the pressure cooker become spoken but only in jest.

The pressure cooker in life is also similar.

Once, what appeared to our demise, now in turn becomes the life that we have never experienced. The only necessity was a change in perception. However, for reasons unspecified here, it does not produce the change. The changes are possible. Everyone's life is a constant pressure cooker designed to produce something totally marvelous, something completely spectacular, edible and delicious. An uncomfortable notion, noted, not all steps are the right steps when taken if proper instructions while in preparation are not ascribed to. It becomes one of the most ridiculous moments ever. Nothing needed was missed, only the instructions given in preparation were not followed.

I had a long gracious conversation with my second oldest son as we were seated eating in at a restaurant. Our conversation was such that my son blessed me. He is such a smart and savvy young man. He's my son. The one thing that struck a chord was the fact that he repeated back to me in a statement that I had spoken moments earlier, is that we often 'take the long way home'! This was just a statement as we discussed various subjects that only a father and a son can, but this one sentence returns to mind as I share with the world in this chapter. Power that is contained in the 'Pressure' cooker is what creative people possess, but are not sure how to safely, purposely put it on display. Another dilemma, the contents within require the proper amount of seasoning for palatability. We experiment, but the owner's manual provides safety recommendations. Nothing is as brilliant as following the instructions provided for safe satisfactory product use. Remember, what pressure brings, time provides a song in its place. Time provides creativity of expression for what seems to be out of your league.

If tenacious, truthfully, it is not.

There is nothing more important than movement. Each part of the physical body is geared and designed to move. Whenever this design is altered movement becomes a real-life frustration in no uncertain terms. A host of life's realest moments take forever without the cooperative synapses bodily all firing simultaneously. The central nervous system plays a major part in the body's mechanism of movement and body mechanics. Neurons, cells, blood plasma, blood flow, proper circulation and varying physical activity not only helps but continues support of overall bodily function and support.

Has anyone ever had the experience of a part of your physical body fall asleep? If you have experienced this, it is brutal if the physical warning signs exist and are intentionally dismissed. The weird sensations begin to manifest where a body part cannot be moved, no this is not a stroke or permanent paralysis. All of this occurs due to delayed movement, pressure place upon a certain part of the body for an overextend amount of time and presto; body parts fall asleep, not a 'Step'!

CHAPTER 8

THE LITERALNESS OF AUTHENTICITY

Questions which are long overdue arise when this subject is presented. This is a hackers' paradise especially if you're a note keeper and all of your personal, intimate inform is stored somewhere in cyberspace. As we have become more and more advance technologically so have our fears of either being exposed or found out in the least to not be who we say that we are or have presented ourselves as being. Friendships end often over new information discovered, so do lifelong marital relationships. Jobs both corporate and otherwise take great measures to discover secrets when attempting to dissolve/downsize curtailing their liabilities to compensate whom they've dismissed without reason. Laughter with persons thought to be trustworthy only comes as a retort of personal exposure. Seemingly, our world has become very cold, and very cruel. When it has been determined that loyalty, allegiance and integrity are not on the playing grounds of life, more cruelty is exposed and experienced. Multiple realities set in as questions surround your thought life considering the literalness of authenticity.

Quite certain, thoughts of how much is too much to share with someone that you do not know; whom you have just met.

Attempting to avoid certain questions or subjects based upon just becoming acquainted with the person justifies the hesitation that you're experiencing. If you have experienced life at any level, you're smart enough to shut up and keep quiet hopefully. Feeling guilty nor experiencing guiltiness should not be an encounter or experience. We all have the right to be quiet until you've acquired correct information of the who the new acquaintance is, the why you are being asked.

Giving any information to the wrong person; your words exactly

Transparency is not an option.

Transparency is a model of excellence acquired through

trust. To not be transparent does not indicate something is being hidden, it only notes that you are not trusted/you are not known well enough to 'trust'!

It is very ignorant, immature, and an ignoble thing to just walk up to someone that you do not know and begin to freely give them access to your life. This is a strange undertaking in which many people are partaking. It is illegitimate transparency. Nothing is proven, there are no steps taken to know if they are trustworthy, although, they are given this level of trust that only comes with time. Not having anything to hide is an often-stated misconception started as a conversation piece, but it is not the wisest piece to begin conversation. If you are an individual of prominence you are often under scrutiny. The scrutiny that you are often subjected to does not leave room for much error. The minutest error is as though you have set off trapdoor alarms, while you are taken hostage. To your chagrin this hostage situation immediately goes viral. It now takes to the worldwide web, social media, with unfounded accusations, and no proof, but you're accused.

Your day has immediately turn into a media frenzied circus.

Being conspired against with information personally that has freely been made public by you is dangerous. The information used is not provided by others. Until you are sure in whom you're confiding is as confidentially adept as the information provided do not provide personal information until the individual has proven authenticity trustworthy over time.

Character not proven does not provide the best proof for transparency ~ Chief Apostle M.III~

Frivolity or light conversation which is informative does not always give clear guidance to what's next. No conversation should ever be noted as just being light conversation. Some individuals' motives are to only gather to scatter when an adequate amount of information personally is received. Individuals who disseminate what you've shared as though it is only running water should not be confided in nor trusted. Frivolity takes place thoughtlessly although others are fully aware of the intents of being frivolous.

There is no such thing as light conversation.

Every conversation informs.

Whenever conversations are laced as trivial, the conversations do not downplay the weight of information released, even if the information given is unintentional.

There will always be moments when your depth of transparency outweighs your literalness of authenticity.

This does not contradict either position, the occurrence is normal. There are many presumptions to base this upon. Hypothetical situations boggle the mind so profusely that transparency becomes distant. The distance that takes place is the constant betrayal experienced at each level where transparency was undermined. Periodically there is a need to reevaluate close relationships making sure that your close inner circle is really as close and as competent as assumed or presumed. If your inner circle takes a direct hit from libelous slander, money laundering or sexual indiscretion it will unravel quicker than a piece of faulty merchandised material.

The need of solidarity is a place of trusted vulnerability maintained among those who have proven themselves, safe, reliable and trustworthy. ~ Chief Apostle M.III~

Desperation appears as though it will permeate the very pores of your being.

This not only causes disgust, emotions are forced to surface. Being devastated is a disaster within itself, to only find out that there is more scheduled. This seems like a soliloquy but it is nothing more than a silhouette masking the restful sounds attempting to block your tranquility.

How can desperation be so cruel when life has been so kind?

It is the same irritant that forces pearls from within oysters/mollusks. Just when you thought that it was safe to return to the waters, you changed. The change is the increase of your personal worth. Instead of being irritated, transparency surfaced as priceless pearls through irritants while intubated.

An intubation stage is not a bad idea.

While being intubated, being intubate has afforded protection. Unknown, things are really working out for you. Although greatly criticized and being investigated, alliances are being formed as key witnesses in your defense. Somehow, you will never ever have to convince anyone of your honesty or of your impeccable character and integrity. The system that was designed to discredit or destroy you must publicly acknowledge your credibility expunging your records in the process of all charges. Every accusation presented does not carry credibility.

There are certain legal proceedings which are enforced without question. The legal proceedings that are conducted are conducted to clear the charges that are presented as true. For some this would be a great time to take advantage of the law to clear your family name. From a legal point of view an amazing array of events are possible as law enforcement and the legal profession attest to your credibility. If certain accusations are presented. i.e. as criminal charges; it is an honor to have those with whom the community holds in high esteem as being credible enough to affirm your credibility. Often doors that were closed, open effortlessly. No need for anxiety exists you're cleared.

Credibility open doors.

The level of credibility that's personally exuded gives access to otherwise inaccessible places and persons that are not accessible. An important note: do not crush nor curse your access. Crushing and cursing your credibility happens through a lack of credible resources and a lack of credibility. Great accomplishments get you noticed but credibility keeps you noticed. It is important to understand subsequently with being noticed, you will need consistency. Nothing ever fails. Failure takes place when preparation does not. Failure is not final; failure is an opportunity.

Credibility presents constant opportunities.

If the opportunities that are constantly presented are forfeited credibility becomes questionable, possibly forfeiting credibility. So how do we exchange what is necessary in order to receive? Credibility forces each person to take the personal credibility assessment. So often downtime in life is a scheduled event. This is fortunately for some, but is very unfortunate for others. Downtime gives the opportunity to reassess motives as well as to correct personal character flaws. I understand that most would prefer to continue as they are and to not address certain personal deficiencies. The difficulty lies in not addressing or dealing with what is prevalent. What remains unaddressed becomes more visible to you and those that you associate, engage and interact with over time. Very few people will find it their responsibility to coddle you by taking you aside in a timely manner to address what is openly visible. The individual that does such should be highly commended. They have considered you important enough to check you.

Great credibility presupposes integrity. ~ Chief Apostle M.III~

In certain moments, it appears that anything other than credibility and integrity will suffice. The statement is not only a faulty one, but it is also fictitious holding no truth. The statement of anything other than credibility and integrity will suffice can be misunderstood and considered as libelous language. Nothing factual can come of this. In moments of great duress, we may consider shortcuts or avenues that appear prominent and prestigious but are duplicitous.

In choosing ignoble directives as an effort to safely get ahead or to arrive quicker, suddenly those opportunities evaporate into thin air as though they were a mirage. To our chagrin now they're totally embarrassing and completely outlandish.

The people who choose to be accountable accomplish their goals. The accountability helps keep them safe. Often corporations, businesses, marriages, friendships, ministries, churches, athletes, actors, doctors and lawyers would have remained innocent, only if they had reliable, trusted sources. Confiding in people who cannot be trusted can be a lifelong lonely road. There will come a time in life where this will become your greatest desire or your greatest need. An intellectuals greatest fear is the fear of being alone. The degree of an 'Intellectuals' success cannot mask the height of an intellectual's fear of being alone. Wealthy individuals pay for the company of other people for many personal reasons. The greatest reason being, to not be 'Alone'. Opportunists take great advantage of such vulnerability and aloneness. Very saddening! ~ Chief Apostle M.III~

Success, but shared with whom? With no one to share, is a prescription for madness and borderline insanity. Although you pride yourself in your accomplishments, others applaud, but you are all alone, having no sense of belonging.

 Are the things that have caused your greatness, now, also the things that have caused you your greatest 'failure'?

Have the things that you have secured, now securing your demise? Has the fame that you have now attained turned and defamed you?

Success means many things to many people, truer success is defined by each person, one person at a time. Being successful at being you is the one of the most successful ventures ever undertaken. Very few people have ever become successful enough to take advantage of being themselves, everyone would prefer to be someone other than who they are. Images only look good, there's a price to pay for an image only.

At the very moment, you are attempting to play copycat, you lose yourself. For some years pass, for others a complete lifetime passes without ever realizing that the person that they have become is the person that they were never determined to be. For years they have played imagery. Their image became imaginary, the imagined themselves as being someone admired greatly by them of whom their imagination carried and captured so deeply they began to detest the very person that they were created to be losing a greater essence that was so original. To admire and to emulate is normal, however that person that you admire so deeply, to become them is never possible.

So many have succeeded at great accomplishments, possessing the accolades that accompany their success, never succeeding at being 'themselves' (The Literalness of Authenticity). It is not a code word!

CHAPTER 9

TWENTY TIMES MORE

Percentages are an 'Investors' calculated concerns. What are the returns upon this investment and what will it yield me? A Diversified Portfolio is a wealthy persons' dream investment. Each area of the market is concerned with limited risk.

Typically, the cow is milked but not drained.

What is 'Twenty Times More"?

Twenty times more is an investment angle, it is not stated to be a hundred times more, but twenty times more.

Twenty is a multiple of tens, fives, fours, twos and ones. It is fascinating when factors are presented as sums, the sum of a product or a finished equation. Twenty is also a whole number which sends us into a totally different category numerically. This awesome perspective of the use of numbers is a marvel within itself.

Every number has a mathematical category, even the alphabets are numeric and numerically arranged. The alphabetical use of numbers, they are indicated throughout certain calculus, algebra, trigonometry, geometry and other scientific sources. In every nation and country all around the globe economics, economic terms are readily admissible to stimulate that nations gross capital economically. This occurs through numbers. No country or economic growth can be sustained without numbers. Each country's sustainability is directly related to numbers. i.e. financial, population or otherwise is only sustained through numeric/numbers.

When dealing with numbers, numbers quickly escalate in whatever form of currency that is related to that country or nations economic acceptance for barter, trade, exchange. The country with the most economic collateral works up the terms of economic exchange and the rules of the same. Weaker countries and nations are identified as those without the collateral for economic exchange thereby becoming in some terms pawns in the hands of wealthier nations and countries to be bullied and pushed around at will based upon their inability to produce recognizable or acceptable resources of wealth.

Economic sanctions are designed to not only punish violators but the economic sanctions are also set in place to cause lesser countries and nations to become dependent upon countries or nations that withhold and uphold them economically. The inability of markets to influence barter and exchange spells unequivocal disaster for nations around the world. At every point, the numbers must be in.

Surplus, the existence of 'Surplus' is undeniable. Without surplus deficits will prevail. The markets are based on a numeric system. The transition within the numeric system are recognized as capital. Capital transitions into wealth, Wealth in turn transitions into currency, currency is what we currently use as a form of monetary exchange/purchasing power called 'Paper Money'.

However, 'Paper Money is one of the lowest forms of economic exchange. Assets are multiple in their variations of expression.

There are many forms of recognizable wealth. The wealth that we have been conditioned to is 'paper money with certain denominations ascribed'. Paper Money/Legal Tender is given legal transaction being noted by the 'denominations' establishing current value'. We use other forms of wealth which are without an ascribed 'denomination paper placement value' such as gold, black gold/oils, diamonds, jewels and pearls to name only a few. All pockets are not silver lined or born with silver spoons in their mouths, but something differing.

Something different is happening. They are born with 'Twenty Times More'!

The talent plus performance ratio is illogical. Performances from this "New Generation After" skills are on a totally different scale altogether. Through literal blood, sweat and tears significant individuals laid the present groundwork from which the current generations are catapulting from.

This is a gifted opportunity.

Gifted opportunities can be forfeited.

Forfeiting gifted opportunities begins with disregarding the correct information and dismissing the right instructions given for excellence. Generations are behind times in innovation because of opportunities forfeited when freely presented. At whatever point in time that uncertainty blocks viewpoints and visions, gifted opportunities are and will be taken for granted. The statement 'Twenty Times More' does not appear to be enough, although two 'twenties' equates to 'forty'.

This alone requires complete stewardship tested before advancing.

Giving understanding to this 'Twenty Times More' reflects 'Redemption' as the number 'twenty' is used but when doubling this number (20) times two, it gives us/becomes the number 'forty'.

The number 'forty' represents three significant things.

However, not in the order written, here are the three things that the number 'forty' represents:

The first.

(1). Testing

The second.

(2). Trials

The third.

(3). Probation

Constantly reflecting is not always a bad habit, it is a good discipline. The often reflections are a simple reminder of the investments that you have made. This keeps you focused on other investments that you have paid into or purchased. Each investment should never be ill advised. Many times, little things which are taken for granted will diminish your ability of acquiring wealth. Not being able to perceptively discriminate what has value and what doesn't create value can decimate everything considered important. To transition from a deficit into acquiring substantial resources, decisions are and will be the primary reasons for increase. No decisions, no increase. Remember, this is not about risk, this is only about making a decisive decision, to increase. Interpretive Financing is a wonderful idea. How does interpretive financing work? Interpretive financing begins with diagnosing a need based upon its vision perspective while allowing the visionary to interpret its perspective as it is underwritten and financed. Creating new visuals and models in the earth creates sustenance. Increasing your substantial aid or assistances, your money levels, takes your clientele to levels of excellence not experienced. Purposely expecting increase without taking the necessary steps only leads to some unknown residual source. Although temporary findings seem paramount enough, they are not enough, residual maybe but not enough,

The 'Times More Factor' must be applied!

How can I stipulate the agreement of terms; the total is arrived at based upon the denominator. A foundation or a support system must be put in place to arrive at the right destination and the correct answer. Any support system that cannot support its weight is not a good support system.

Systems fail based upon overload.

Have you ever heard of the term 'circuit overload' or 'systems overload'? The overload principle establishes the fact that not another thing can be handled or added. However, with this principle of 'Twenty Times More', there is a built in technological surge advance, a serious surge protection being in place to safely navigate any overload.

Having a perfect system designed to navigate is wonderful, experiencing an all-out overload is better. There are times that certain demarcations are subject to tests. Allowing yourself a special liberty to find out what does 'Twenty Times More' feels like and looks like.

Many times, experiential reservations continue you exactly where you are. No this is not about risk. This is about creating a you that has never been, developing, increasing, expanding, leaving your comfort zone, without fear. Experiencing a completely new relevance, is an ideal whose time has come. It is like being afraid to safely jump, with every protective harness attached and a comrade comes along and sternly, strongarms and pushes you off and away from where you were frozen, lifelessly. The adrenaline begins pumping profusely as your heart races, pounding, you shriek in fear. The flushness of your skin pours with perspiration as your pores open, sweating.

Your heart becomes like a little chatter box, coining all your phrases while telling all your secrets, hidden agendas, stories and all. There's new evidence, traces, stories, as you realize, that this more scenario is the bomb, for sure, for real. Are there real fantasies to be fulfilled? Wait there is more, multiplicitous more. What's obvious, is the fact, there are no more options.

It's going to be so good, that it gets better. A rush to judgement is not all that it appears, it can be insidious, libelous, and slanderous. All the evidence, possibly isn't as factual as presented, and who knows, who wants who knocked off. Character assassinations are a dime a dozen when it comes to payoffs. People generally do not care about if the person is innocent when bribed. The life live has been a struggle, what is viewed is an opportunity to get ahead, morality is not considered. Statements based upon opportunity are given to remain in the clear without being found guilty. Somehow, the conscience has a way of catching up with you in more ways than one. Health begins to fail as the physical body implodes under the weight of guilt, dishonor and dishonesty.

The picture becomes completely sadden if memory loss becomes a leading component in the descent because of not being able to confess and free the mind of its impending doom of mental incarceration. Whenever your mind is caught guilty, under duress, arrested with deep charges of the soul, what do you do. When given an analysis it all stalemates, nothing more to say, state or to give. Conversations end without knowing the reasons why. Speculations occur, no answers given. Accusations ensue, criminal charges based upon being in the wrong place at the wrong time; the suspect analysis. It is normally stated that you are innocent until proven guilty, but this time you're guilty, a suspect, nothing proven, without trial, no jury, only one person, accusing you.

Such reputation precedes the interpretation of process, one person, with that much judicial gall, the others totally shrink away in fear. Intimidation, that is what this is completely about. The manipulation of the human mind, the hearts palpitating in fear afraid to confront the insidious, asinine logic of this perpetuitous logician. In the life of all of humanity is the impetuous cringe of what is the next step; Frustration arises. Is it a love affair with life that you are after or is it a revelation that frustration brings without your being aware that frustration comes with answers; inconspicuously, yes.

Our constantly being barraged with overload is the factor that presents a different principle not factored into the equation. A perfect percentile of life is equated to both epiphany and revelation. Most epiphanies are revelatory expressing an unrehearsed moment repressed dislodging of information made readily available at a period that you're most in need. Frustration does not bear a loss, it is very opportune. However, frustration always arrives with answers, it never shows up empty handed. The only thing that is irreversible is your life, but what underscores this, is that you and your life are protected.

Every expletive is not only damning, they are demeaning or threatening with a projected recourse. As the "Twenty Times More" concept permeates your being with its own thought life, find it, work it, protect it, favor it and never settle for less than more. Your personal focal point has interwoven perspectives awaiting, protect them. The persons that you kick it with, be certain that their perception cooperates with your overall objective maintaining your focus. Never place people in a position of authority who choose to be contentious against your perspective; regarding more, especially, not "Twenty Times More". Your present dilemma has placed you in a beautiful position, think about it, you're in for more than you've ever bargained for; Get it, take it, Receive it!

CHAPTER 10

STOPPED IN THE MIDDLE OF THE ROAD

Have you ever?

This is the paradigm shifter.

How does it feel to stop or to be stopped smack dad in the middle of the road, full of busy commuters, with everyone going from zero to a hundred, and you're the one who has traffic held up for miles?

Your vehicle has completely stopped, not a thing within or on your vehicle is responding and for whatever crazy reason it stopped as you were preparing to turn off of a main thoroughfare in midstride. The automobile that you were driving stopped, blocking every lane of oncoming traffic.

Every vehicle on the road is now completely at a standstill, horns blasting and blaring. People are using full sentence expletives. The expletives are being hurled in your direction, specifically at you. The angry mob appears to assemble to draw blood or to take life away.

Quickly, life changes as many individuals get out of their vehicles to see why the traffic has come to a complete halt. Angry, swearing, overheated, hot on a strangely strange summers day, automobiles overheating during the length of the stalled traffic, babies screaming to the top of their lungs either because their hot, soiled or wet diapers are now in need of being changed. No restrooms or places to relieve themselves, people begin to be barbaric resorting back to nature doing whatever being distressed and displaced, completely inconvenienced at this moment. For some unknown reason, you're at peace, not even a hint of perspiration nor a glistening of sweat. As everyone rushes into your direction, you sit and you smile attempting to know when to say what as each person gets closer.

The whole scenario is almost idiomatic, totally cerebral. Everyone now looks in disgust, completely in astonishment. It is your next action that you take that leaves everyone almost breathless. This mob is intense, intensely insane. But you stand, breathless while exhaling as this next screen filters through your lips, everyone pauses, gaping and gasping for air as one by one they clutch their chest over their hearts. A song begins to float on the air through pursed lips, the melodious lyrics of:

Stop! In the Name of Love by Diana Ross

Stop! In the name of love

Before you break my heart

Baby, baby

I'm aware of where you go

Each time you leave my door

I watch you walk down the street

Knowing your other love, you'll meet

But this time before you run to her

Leaving me alone and hurt

(Think it over) After I've been good to you?

(Think it over) After I've been sweet to you?

Stop! In the name of love

Before you break my heart

Stop! In the name of love

Before you break my heart

Think it over

Think it over

I've known of your

Your secluded nights

I've even seen her

Maybe once or twice

But is her sweet expression

Worth more than my love and affection?

But this time before you leave my arms

And rush to her charms

(Think it over) haven't I been good to you

(Think it over) haven't I been sweet to you

Stop!...

Breathlessness, as everyone does the hustle in the streets, teary-eyed, excited and in need of Kleenex.

Such exuberance, such enthusiasm, from this 'Stopped in The Middle of The Road', roadside Karaoke crisis on display. Someone shouts out loud hey, sing that again, as others erupt into vociferous laughter. People now stand without hostility having been completely disarmed by the actual even which moments ago transpired. Others laugh as they begin making their way back to their stranded, scattered park vehicles. They're now wearing smiles that they were not capable of when they were suddenly introduced to an inconvenience which that sensed to be of catastrophic proportions an hour before.

It is amazing how an inopportune period or time can be altered by the lyrics of a song. The right song and the right chords of music often catapult and overthrow, while overturning everything. In a quick glance, questions arise, what happened to the problem, where did the frustration.

Frustration cannot keep or maintain company with an uninvited song, sound or chords of music for which it has no appetite or thirst nor thrust for. Frustration can only remain where it is invited or given an invitation. The problem becomes magnified once an invite or an invitation has been given to frustration. Frustration can only drive as far as it is fueled or for as long as its battery source is powered. There are some things that frustration has presented, that you must pull the plug on and let it die.

Die it must; Stopped. In the Middle of The Road!

Once the things that have given life to situations are recognized, do not call for it to be towed, finding itself in other stages of your life. Let the dead bury the dead and do not attempt to revive nor resuscitate.

Anything that has ceased to function has ceased to function or to continue for a reason. There is a difference in a momentary pause and a complete stop. One is designed for rest and the other is scheduled to continue no longer.

How often does it take for you to be stopped in the middle of the road before you realize, maintenance is required or that you should not be required to continue being stopped or stranded in wrong areas of travel? i.e. such as hoods that are not neighbor friendly or streets where you could end up dead. Swimming upstream; Oh Really?

Well maybe oh Mike can help you with that. Come here Michael!

Michael row the boat ashore, Hallelujah

Michael row the boat ashore, Hallelujah

Sister help me to trim the sails, Hallelujah

Sister help me to trim the sails, Hallelujah

Jordan's river is deep and wide, Hallelujah

And I've got a home on the other side, Hallelujah

Michael row the boat ashore, Hallelujah

Michael row the boat ashore, Hallelujah

Michael's boat is a music boat, Hallelujah

Michael's boat is a music boat, Hallelujah

Michael row the boat ashore, Hallelujah

Michael row the boat ashore, Hallelujah

The trumpets sound the jubilee, Hallelujah

The trumpets sound for you and me, Hallelujah

Michael row the boat ashore, Hallelujah

Michael row the boat ashore, Hallelujah

Michael row the boat ashore, Hallelujah

Michael row the boat ashore, Hallelujah

Song: Ole Negro Spiritual

Some things are pacified if they are not disturbed, others will never be pacified even if not disturbed. Letting dead dogs to lie out without a burial does not cease or stop the decomposition process nor the stench of decaying flesh when blown by the wind. If there are times, and there will be, when nothing ceases to amaze. If you go to the direct opposite side of the room, clearly away from everyone with the intent of not disturbing anyone, every person in the same room will make it a point to find themselves completely shoulder to shoulder with you, while three fourths of the room remain vacant, completely unoccupied.

How is it that everyone wants to get so close, now?

With much consideration, you were. attempting to respect other people's personal space. The intent was to not crowd the space of others, your space was just completely overtaken with people who decided to gather in your special little cubicle and private space uninvited. Somehow, this seemed to be more of a conspiracy if anything or maybe not. Maybe, it's your cologne or maybe it's the perfume that you are wearing, that states, come, approach me, crowd me if your wish.

In other words, could you be just that dashing, just that

striking, that the atmosphere of your persona compels people to not only get close but to crowd your space completely and to follow you and your every move? For some reason, you are not irked by all this crowd. The imbalance created in a room challenging the architectural structure design with everyone only being on one side of the room, the weight sustained speaks volumes

Apparently, I'm certain that you are shocked, stopped in the middle of the room, thinking, hey, wait a minute, maybe you begin singing, harmoniously harmonizing while humming "Deborah Cox's" potently, powerful, Love Ballad.

Come here 'Deborah', sing 'Girl'.

Deborah Cox Lyrics

Nobody's Supposed to Be Here

{Chorus}

How did you get here?

Nobody's supposed to be here

I've tried that love thing for the last time

My heart says no, no!
Nobody's supposed to be here
But you came along and changed my mind
I've spent all my life, on a search to find
The love who'll stay for eternity

143

The heaven sent to fulfill my needs

But when I turn around

Again, love has knocked me down

My heart got broken, oh, it hurt so bad

I'm sad to say, love wins again

So, I placed my heart under lock and key

To take some time, and take care of me

But I turn around and you're standing here

{Chorus}

This time I swear I'm through

But if only you knew

How many times I've said those words

Then fall again, when will I ever learn

Knowing these tears, I cry

This lovely black butterfly

Must take a chance, and spread my wings

Love can make you do some crazy things

So, I placed my heart under lock and key

To take some time, and take care of me

But I turn around and you're standing here

{Repeat chorus to fade}

When life has only afforded and offered you only painstaking unformidable realism as your reality, stressed out situations that seem to real to be true and moreover, frustration that never seems to leave nor go away. You personally feel like you have been to the primordial soup box, hatchet ridden to no end, and now this. Life has an amazing way of not being as it is presented or appears. You're ready to completely give up, not knowing what's ahead nor the relevant opportunities waiting for you to clear that very last obstacle on your life's course.

This seems like the hurdle that just will not go away.

It not only appears that you are stopped, but you are 'stop stuck'! Where you are now, seems like, not only, what happened, but 'who happened'.

Handling fallen things, think twice before you attempt to catch things that are falling. Once you reach for falling things, catching them in a position that challenges your proper body balance can injure you. Think of a heavy object falling. As the heavy object falls, you reach for the object without thought, the object pulls you into the direction of its fall, unrealized is the immediate misaligning of your physical body based upon the weight of the object being caught. The object snatches your body with such force and gravitational pull. Seconds later, an unnoticed twinge of pain pulsates throughout your body. The pain being experienced when the object was caught completely stopped you in the middle of an action.

Pain was not a factor, pain was introduced.

Writhing in pain is not a happy occasion for anyone. Fallen things, based upon where they fall or are place will determine if passage is possible. The things in your path can summon your attention while endangering you at the very same time. Should you find yourself picking up fallen things, consider what you are picking up attempting to place into position.

How has the fall damaged what you are attempting to place into position again?

The damaged that the fallen object has incurred can vary according to the height or the depth of its fall. There are certain factors that must be taken into consideration.

If you are caught with the fallen possession/object in your possession will you be accused as though you were taking the object, i.e. purloining perhaps? There are many reasons to be stopped in the middle of something, being stopped in the middle of the road is very serious. Being stopped by law enforcement can be major or it can be minor, it is based upon the reason of being stopped.

The only reason you have the object in hand is to place it in its proper position and placement, again.

Once you have placed the fallen thing into position again, is it able to maintain its position without falling again or the need to be caught or repositioned. Many times, we play the savior only to find out that what has fallen, falls again knowing that there is someone to reposition it into position. There is a great element of love staged and patience portrayed upon this fallen object of great affection, this priceless object. An object that has learned the art of stoppage with the ability to pull upon the heartstrings at will, stopping everything and everyone in their tracks.

Great personal perspectives are developed.

It is now, that things are drawn out. Things that place motives, objectives, whims and desires are clearly seen. Other things previously unknown play out. Stop, take a moment to assess everything. If a slightly hesitant perspective is taken to stabilize before decisions are made, your moment to assess will not alter anything. Rushing to rescue, is not the best advice when fallen things have come with an agenda. This does not remove your sensitivity nor does it take away your being able to be sensitive in/to an actual emergency. In the middle of the road you are stopped. Everything within you is hollering, screaming, shouting and for some, you're cussing at the top of your voice. You are afraid!

Everything within you is heightened, every nerve, every fiber of your being. There has never been a moment like this.

Your scared is scared and even your fear is fearful, your tears have tears in their eyes, but the tears are not tears of remorse, hurt or regret. The tears are tears of power, tears of great resolve. Instead of considering the stop in the middle of the road, a quick glance has determined that I'm not dying today nor the next.

Everything will stop, as it all waits, for you; Remember:

Stop! In the Name of Love

Diana Ross Lyrics

{Chorus}

Stop! In the name of love

Before you break my heart

POWER IN THE PRESSURE COOKER FRUSTRATION

CHAPTER 11

NOTE, NOTATION(S) AND NOTEWORTHY

There are many things in life, which would not be worth the note quickly scribbled note. The notation(s) placed as a bookmark, marking a milestone accomplishment, the milestone accomplishment considered, may not be of a noteworthy cause. The things noted are known as the unmentionables.

Each moment in life self-dictates. The self-dictation of every moment comes under constant speculation if close attention is given. Certain levels of consternation are all a part of life, it does not portray life as being all evil.

This should be noted.

Taking notes and keeping short accounts should never be an option. Whenever notes are not taken or kept complexity arises. Attempting to commit so many things to memory only complicates things more. Everyone has experienced this at some time, only to end up at the conclusion that it does not work. As fast paced as life is, please commit to notetaking. Sure, everything isn't worth the ink or the cyberspace function on a smart device unless in your world you value it. The constant barrage of an impressionist's agenda can cause anyone to not expend the energy to notate anything, as noteworthy.

During this, values would be enacted.

What's it worth to you?

Is there an accurate assessment placed as how to determine what to consider important, and if so, where do we begin? It is mind boggling how encumbered we can become without realizing that what we have just taken on as an assignment was never ours to begin with. It was only a good idea or a need that needed fulfillment. You remember, somebody's got to do it, why not you, why not me. As noble as such dialogue is, it does not state that you are assigned for this or to do. Being pugnacious and not understanding the difference in being tenacious is a nightmare.

Nightmares are not like the coolest things to sleep with or on. No, you cannot sleep with or on a nightmare, silly you.

Let's do a quick assessment, an evaluation, a mini test or lesson assignment.

When it is critical and a need to recall certain things that are critically important without a 'note (not the 'Samsung Note'), are you available to remember exactly where you placed your last note, without notating the notation(s) of where you placed it? Honestly, you thought that it was in a worthwhile, noteworthy area.

Taking mental notes can lead to great speculation, don't forget the stress of forgetfulness. Forgetfulness is based upon prioritization, notate this just for notes sake. Anything that is meaningful or vitally important does not get categorized into the forgetful compartment or the department store mental dismissal isle to be returned to the shelf, only to be lost (forgotten) again.

Ah, is this being duly noted?

Documentation of every event of importance is a great place to begin notations while taking notes and making what is valuable to you memorable. Special moments and important information should never be given to chance. The moments and the information are too important to casually glance over but to not prioritize. Each sitting require tact. If things are not tactful nor tactfully completed, it is certain to cause uprising of possible heated proportions that are not easily addressed or dismissed. Times that were lost find themselves wishing that the moments would be represented all over again, once more.

Hypotheticals do not work when things are no longer just the possible permissible presentation of would be markets, marketers and buyers once things are all too surreal.

Keeping records of live births as well as deaths are all too obvious and the need is not to be speculated when each one truly matters. If we get away from the obvious we lose sensitivity unless the obvious is completely unhealthy. Birthdates are remembered, the height and weight are also remembered especially of small children and many adolescents, even those who are attempting to begin any type of health or fitness regimen. Nothing goes without being recognized. Everything is noted at least by some thing or by someone somewhere sight unseen.

Take this small test.

Sitting anywhere or any place without thinking, you're taking notes, making notation(s) of your surroundings. The things/the people capture your attention. There are those standout moments you put on subconscious pause, play, repeat moments effortlessly without notice. This is a description of capturing a snapshot of something noteworthy.

The actions portrayed or laid out in certain environments are really real and at some point, could endanger you, your life or otherwise could spare you, your life and others. There is nothing that can come close to being able to recognize not only your surroundings but the atmospheres that your surroundings alert you of and portray.

This takes notetaking unto a totally unheard-of arena.

What is customary is the taking of notes, the court recorder, the dictation of notes by a secretary in an office, boardroom meeting, private meetings. The awareness of the technologically advanced age that we are currently ascribed is completely mindboggling. Devices receive and transmit information without anyone being aware of the incidental/intentional dissemination of that information without permission. The documentation of social medias notes, and notation(s) of every word spoken, every word uttered or the physical/non-physical expression of others that captivate audiences are now subject to their discretion and depiction of what is considered noteworthy.

Possessing anything that has great value always adds greater value to the person that possesses it. Do you possess anything of great value that you have not purchased? It is important that you know what you possess having not purchased.

A Family Heirloom

A Family Heirloom constitutes great value, although the pricelessness of the 'Heirloom' may not be considered to possess any value. When things/possessions are being valued, things that are valued are only recognized to be of great value if they have been appraised. Appraisal value is not always based upon markets. An appraised value can also be constituted according to sentimental value of the possessor. This goes along with property, houses, land, vehicles, furnishings, paintings, books, pictures and a host (conglomerate) of other otherwise non-essentials that holds no value to anyone but the possessor.

Time is always a valuable commodity, completely priceless. Once time is used properly, the proper use of time amasses and acquires great wealth with success, successfully. Each person has the same amount of time delegated. The purpose of delegation, reflectively, to delegate is to deputize with authority; the right to use power authoritatively. This should only be conducted with the assurance and the authorization from whomever has authorized the use of authority. Considering time being priceless we labor with time in mind knowing that certain dividends are in place for compensation once the time allotted has been fulfilled.

Seasons must not only be anticipated, but seasons must be acknowledged. Seasons consist of periods of calculated time. Calculated time presents certain events that are scheduled to occur to fall on specific days, dates along with the arranged times. It is best to acknowledge the well know euphemism, that timing is everything.

Certain repetitive occurrences present themselves habitually. They are presented repeatedly without question, no hesitation. Every repetitive occurrence is not a dreaded, dreadful event. There are some things in life that need an invocation of acceptance with arms wide open. Personal perspectives must adjust to time, timing, and make the adjustment of seasonal perspectives. Often a perspective is incorrect based upon the lenses used to view. An appropriate view using lenses would be the view of respect. Respecting perspectives, is not an implied stating that the perception viewed is correct. The disagreeable view point only states, that it presents a moment for a different perspective to quickly adjust their lenses, if necessary, reevaluating while perhaps clearing the view for agreement.

Reevaluating a general perspective comes with total openness while being pliable. If all parties involved are set in their perspective view, nothing gets resolved. Most sight positions are only set through life experiences. Every life experience is not bad, dramatic or traumatic. For some, things become very complicated if the opposite has been experienced. Let's get back to seasons being acknowledged.

Note, Notation(s) and Noteworthy.

I'm completely certain, better yet, I'm positive, that you have taken literal notes within while being stretched by this subject, and rightly so. There is nothing greater than the right perspective, covering everything in life, Frustration included.

Without 'Vision' there is no 'Drive'! We are referring to the correct vision, properly actuated, enhanced and applied. "Where's your Vision"!?

It is possible to be motivated but not actuated. Motivation can be short lived, however, not so with being actuated. One can be stated as being the fuel, the other the actual 'Fire'. Drive is needed, the motivation to get your vision to the right location.

This is actuation, to be literally actuated. The word play upon the words motive, motivate, motivation, motivated, active, activity, activate, activated, activation, actuate, actuation, actuated seem similar but the emphasis of the active participle changes everything. Word semantics, the origin of words in their full meaning with their original intent can change the very way words are viewed. Motion sensors detect movement, alerting that physical presence is detected or has been sensed by the sensors, at other times it maybe debris or wind picked up by your protective home, vehicle or office device. It never hurts to be certain of what your sensor devices has detected.

At all times, be sure to check, to be safe. Take a moment to survey your surroundings, become very familiar with where you live, also know the things that will cause a false alarm by triggering your protective device. Be certain to move anything that can cause your sensors to trigger if possible otherwise if they are not moveable, note them.

The mindset/the mentality of being reciprocal as well as

experiencing the principle of reciprocation cannot be obtained if nothing leaves your life (your possession).

Reciprocating is based upon things leaving your life first; i.e. Principles of Sowing and Reaping, Seedtime and Harvest.

Wealth comes because of the above principles being adhered to while measurably put into consistent practice.

Are you planning to get, are you planning to receive? As a rule of thumb before getting or receiving, first plan to give, the getting gets easy and the receiving comes without complication(s).

If you are an individual that has a difficult time receiving, you are a violator of 'Principle(s)' and you are a "Harvest Terrorist". You have sown into the cycle of Harvest with your giving, but you refuse to receive.

Such is false 'Humility', now receive!

Note this, consider it a Notation worth the Notations of keeping with consistency, never to be denied of its Noteworthy nature.

POWER IN THE PRESSURE COOKER FRUSTRATION

CHAPTER 12

STOP!

In greater terms than any human being can ever say; Get Out of My Way!

To you, it appears that this is a difficult season of life, nonetheless, a truer realization is everything that has happened has been allowed. Each event has permission. The permission is either yours or someone other than you who has the authorization.

Things can never not be what you allow.

Forget taking a bow, you are yet, 'Pausing'. Instead of taking a bow, take 'Pausing'! Pausing

When pausing only for a brief second, a moment into your future opens briefly but with only a glimpse of certain possibilities, while you are paused.

This momentary glimpse is often given on a paused moment. There was no intent to reflect, only pausing for a brief second. While paused, you've found yourself thrust into a future glimpse of enormous grandeur, even opulence. Stunned and shocked, you shudder almost speechless, breathless and into shock. It is quickly summed up and dismissed as though you're hallucinating or daydreaming.

The number of times that this place has been entered and walked out of and away from cannot be counted, but accounted for, it can be. Dreams, and visions are there in the puzzled place of pausing, not actually understanding why you decided to pause at the very moment that you have. It is all too familiar now as years of pausing rushes into remembrance. It is years of things known, perceived, viewed and seen of future accomplishments or possessions, but never ever obtained. A belief of I'm only daydreaming or wishing. Such has caused a non-possession of what has been viewed.

Pausing elevates your perception, your level of perceiving becomes more accurately perceptive. A pause is good for the mind. This enhances the ability of gathering and processing information more proficiently. For those of you who have constant mood swings and in you are now in between tirades of emotional outburst, try pausing for a moment before you present another disastrous episode. Begin to closely pay attention to what triggers your outbursts.

Pausing only for a moment can keep arguments from being fueled by words you cannot retract. Hurtful words also destroy worlds. How often have worlds which were being built find themselves in shambles, destroyed in moments. Only if seconds before, the art of pausing were practiced. Who knows how beautiful the worlds would be, if only pausing were at the helm of the ship while sailing along or at the center of the relationship while building. Pausing; a stroke of 'Genius'.

Delay

A slight hold up of plans or arrival.

Delay is not a prediction nor is it a denial. It is not a permanent hold up of what was expected although for most individuals they have taken delay as a permanent action, delaying both their expectation and joyous experience once manifested or received. It is not prophetic nor a prophetic fulfillment to not receive.

Opportunist capitalize on distressed individuals regularly who are experiencing delay. The fearmongers hassle, while others hustle those who fear that things are not going to work out or in their favor. Always keep in mind that this is only a delay. There is no permanence in this momentary situation. If you can seriously calm down and keep your cool the experience will be well worth it. It is only a delay. Finding yourself shortsighted and disgusted over a delay has real consequences. An unrecognized delay can have you overemphasizing everything.

The inability to recognized delayed activity is disastrous.

Nothing is final in a delay. The only thing final regarding a delay, is that, it is, delayed. What normally takes place in a delay is that people begin formulating opinions and thoughts of complete speculation. Drawing conclusions in a moment of delay is evil. Beginning to presume while answering yourself as though the other person is speaking to you is insane. You cannot answer for another person's delay unless you have all the details. i.e. you were there with them when they were delayed. However, this becomes even more impossible to respond for the other person, because you are not the other person, plus their way of processing a delay maybe significantly different than yours.

Stop attempting to destroy your life over something that is delayed.

Remember it is delayed, not denied. If it is delayed, it is delayed for good reason. In all your excitement, you failed to prepare. The level of preparation necessary may require more time. If what you anxiously await is presented before the product is completed, a million years from now you will wish that you had allowed the delay.

It was not a no, it was only a delay.

The delay created a space, although it will arrive as scheduled. Humorously, you will arrive as scheduled also. As for the drama, kill it. Puzzle pieces always annoy those who are into putting the puzzle pieces together. There is that one piece of the puzzle that without fail, appears to be missing. Once the search begins for the missing piece of the puzzle accusations begin forming if you are working together with others and not completing the puzzle alone. Seemingly, everyone is on edge over a piece of cardboard, shaped, colored and presented with a picture image. But there is a piece of the puzzle missing. Have you ever noticed that in life, there is always a piece of the puzzle missing?

Be perfectly assured that the piece of the puzzle that is missing will soon be found or discovered once it is acknowledged as missing. An all-out search ensues for the missing piece. The piece is only temporarily displaced or misplaced. Temporary delay, permanent satisfaction.

Yield

To surrender completely, to give rite of passage or right of way to another.

Serenity, peace, trust

An infectious labor and laboring of love it is, to yield. The value of yielding must have a currency of its own. Nothing is more infectious than to yield. Such sweet surrender that it brings knowing that the responsibility is entrusted to another. Fictitiously, when the one to whom yield has been given knows the way and the terrain treaded.

On the other hand, there are those who defiantly choose to not yield one iota, no, not even an inch. There is no yield, they are unyielded. Nothing in their vocabulary speaks of yielding. They're all in it more specifically, for themselves. To the lake with everybody else, the hot part, no, not the lake with water and the cold frigid temperatures. It is important for them to be first at whatever expense, to be seen, to be heard, to be known, so their statement begins with, don't come here starting with all of that 'yield' stuff.

I'm not giving one inch.

Loud sounds always gather crowds, peak interests, but if it is known that the loud sounds are a setup, many individuals would remain unharmed without the loss of life. Very well, this is not the case. Crowds draw deviants. Not in every crowd is deviancy anticipated nor in every setting. There are some settings where deviancy lurks, waiting to strike. Deviancy often strikes where people are unwary, non-attentive. They are helpless when the inadmissible happens, without being aware of the things that lurk which give no warning. Quietness is often dismissed as a place for deviancy to occur.

In as much as to yield is beautiful, it is just as beautiful to be attentive, knowing to what you yield. Surprisingly, most people who yield are inattentive to whom and to what they yield. Being carefree is one thing, being totally stupid and idiotic is something completely different. People with special needs need people to be aware for them whether they are adults or children. Knowingly yield to persons who are known to be of repute.

Once you yield, rest.

The above is vitally important. It is important that we all learn how to rest. Sleeping does not mean that you are resting, not only that, sleeping does not mean that you are safe. Sleeping signifies that your body is tired and that you did yield in cooperation. However, although you slept, it is possible to awake drained as though you did not sleep. To yield prevents catastrophes of every magnitude.

Little did you know that all of this time, that there were people behind you waiting for you to relinquish the space that you've been sitting, for fifteen minutes, you've been parked at the yield sign!

Detour

Taking a different route to the same destination based upon advisable conditions or conditions not conducive for safety.

This is admissible.

Have you ever taken a detour?

Were you forced to take a detour?

Did the detour put you in a place that you were completely unfamiliar with?

Such are the scenarios of detours, totally dismiss the thought(s) of being late or not being on time. Everything that you have scheduled is now unscheduled and the plans are not going as planned.

Detours take place for many reasons.

However, there are some detours that only can be shared once you have arrived at safety. But there are other detours, which are completely unexplained and are otherwise unexplainable. A key component is that you are not only safe, you are alive and so is everyone that traveled with you. Everyone is completely unharmed. Each person, interpretively, has their very own personal view of what took place, blow by blow.

The moments after taking a detour, the unexplainable facial expression(s) upon each passenger are unforgettable. We've driven through the country, possibly into a bad community where every unmentionable happens. Fears upon fear, trepidation like you have never thought possible grips each person. Their hearts appear to be flatlining. The air is charged with flatulence. Next, someone screams out, I got to go, I've got to go.

Deafening silence!

It is like an equinox, a lunar eclipse, a modern-day flood and thunderstorm combined. A shout from the driver comes out of the silence. 'Are you kidding me'? And like most parents or drivers, their next statement is, can't you hold it? We are in strange, foreign and unknown territory. We are in a region that I know nothing of or about and I know no one, again, no one.

The detour has so many variables that it is mind boggling, even the detour has detours and is not complaining of all the high-end vehicles traveling through. Here is insight. The area traveled has never been traveled. There are details in this area that are worth more than every vehicle that has adventured, passing through the area. Unknown to everyone involved, the detour is a scheduled test attempting to cause conception while staggering the imagination of what is possible within a detour. Every area is virgin, untouched and untapped. The resources that this detour possesses are unknown. Yeah baby, you have taken the scenic route, but what are you seeing or what are you missing being that you are not seeing anything at all.

A trained perception is what you have, however, a trained perception from whose perspective. The detour is impossible to not take or to miss. This detour was mandatory!

If the only thing that you can see is the detour, you are missing the resources.

Stop

Complete nonmovement, but completely attentive to your surroundings.

It is possible to be completely stopped but totally inattentive. The sign that you are facing states stop, choosing not to stop, you have just entered a danger zone. There is nothing more insightful than a ticket for a nonstop if you are driving. The ticket for violation will never be forgotten. From the day of the stop by law enforcement it will be your sworn duty to stop.

Nothing is as foreboding when a vehicle decides to surge through a traffic light that is completely red, the amber light has ceased to be visible. This is ridiculous, without warning, the traffic begins moving in the direction of where the light is green, suddenly, a vehicle speeds through where the traffic light is now red. The screeching sound of tires with brakes engaged, hearts palpitating at a rate of speed that makes Star Trek appear to be slow as the would-be lawbreaker endangers the lives of innocent would be victims. Narrowly the vehicle escapes the danger, everyone is safe, no fatalities, only a few wet seats along with irate drivers swearing to the top of their lungs.

What just transpired was a violation against sanity. Laws, rules, traffic signs, landmarks are all in place for a reason. Some are in place to remind us of the progress that we have made others are there to protect us keeping the torch of progress lit enabling to never regress. Stars are placed into the heavens for reasons to assure direction, the moon for light during the night, the sun as a special force during the day providing what is necessary as does the rain and the snow. The seasons change with specificity engaging the period as each season is scheduled. Creation knows the moments that it is given. The potential for boundary overlaps is substantial, but by an unseen scheduled force, boundaries are accepted, expected, acknowledged, recognized, respected and restored exactly as ordered.

With crass and with sarcasm, what the unseen forces predict and have put in place are violated by those that are somewhat smarter than the elements. No boundaries. Things are not acknowledged, accepted, expected within reason, recognized or respected. This creates fuzziness if a restoration process is attempted. The lines are totally blurred without demarcation.

If in a thousand lifetimes the same law is violated, should you live forever knowing that the same law is intentionally broken?

There are principles that govern every sphere of life, government, and society. Most of the principles are not known. The principles that are known are yet unseen. Although unseen each principle works according to the laws and the rules that govern them. Once they are known, once they are made applicable, once they are practiced lives are saved, people are bettered.

Is frustration your enemy, is it the nemesis of all good, should frustration be banned and outlawed, should frustration never ever be experienced again. If frustration is outlawed all of creation ceases and every ounce of creativity stops. The dark ages are created again and we enter into total complacency.

Stop

Complete non movement, but completely attentive to your surroundings!

Made in the USA
Coppell, TX
14 March 2021

51734730R00095